CHANGING TIMES

To Rachel

CHANGING TIMES

NIGEL GRANT

Copyright © 2014 by Nigel Grant.

ISBN:	Softcover	978-1-4931-3891-3
	Ebook	978-1-4931-3892-0

All rights reserved. No part of this book may be reproduced or transmitted in any form or by any means, electronic or mechanical, including photocopying, recording, or by any information storage and retrieval system, without permission in writing from the copyright owner.

This is a true story based on the author's recollection of his experiences, however some names have been changed to false names to protect the privacy of certain individuals and no malice or insults are intended.

This book was printed in the United States of America.

Rev. date: 01/15/2014

To order additional copies of this book, contact:
Xlibris LLC
0-800-056-3182
www.xlibrispublishing.co.uk
Orders@xlibrispublishing.co.uk

DEDICATION

This is dedicated to my mother, for her special memories and stories, and also to my brothers and sisters who helped me piece the story together and write about my experiences, without repercussions, I hope. With thanks, too, to Carol and Pedie for their input into making this happen.

Chapter 1

This is how I remember growing up. It's a reflection and a true story about my life and the people I've met.

I was born on the thirty first of January nineteen fifty in Morinsh in Glenlivet in a wooden forestry cottage that had been converted from army Nissan huts. The brick foundations were used as the template for the houses, they weren't very big but it was the only new house my mother was ever to live in. There were two cottages, our one was called Glen-Echo. We lived in that one and Uncle Doug and Auntie Elli in the other. As new houses they had inside toilets, a luxury Mum had never experienced before and for her to turn on the bath tap and have instant hot water (well almost instant as the fire had to be on) must have been quite a luxury.

Before that, when my father and mother got married, they lived in Aberlour in a small bed sit and both worked for Walkers the Bakers, now the biggest shortbread makers in the world, Dad as a van driver and Mum in the shop. But after my sister Alison was

Mum and Dad when they got married

born, followed a year later by brother Bob they had to move and that is when they moved to Bankhead Cottage, which didn't have running water. No toilet and no cooking methods. The water had to be carried 100 yards from a spring and the outside toilet got emptied every morning into the passing burn. Hot water came from an enamelled bucket heated up on a primus stove. The same method was used to boil the nappies. As well as living in near poverty they had two children to look after and keep warm—not easy when the fire surround was wood and you could only put on a fire if you were around in case the surround went on fire!

The new house must have been such a luxury, you just can't imagine what it must have been like to go from one extreme to the other, it must have made life so much easier and more enjoyable. Over the next three years Ian and I were born, maybe the new house wasn't such a good idea after all. I don't remember very much about the inside of the house apart from the chair I split my head on when Dad was changing his trousers and I shouted, 'I can see your drawers' and went to run away and tripped over his feet and split my head, and that mark is still there 60 years later.

baby me and Sis

picking my nose

sunny days

cool shorts

smile

Bob and Sis in fashion show

The baths, always on a Sunday night, were a bit of a luxury too, but only one a week in those days, and shared. The range was a multipurpose fire which kept the house warm and was used to cook on, with a built in oven at the side, and it heated the water, even although

Mum still had to go and collect the wood. There was none of this bath every night as kids have nowadays. A bit of dirt never did us any harm and probably gave us a lot more resistance to illness. Children now have no resistance because they are scrubbed so clean using chemicals that kill good bacteria as well as the bad bacteria. We had carbolic soap. It didn't smell very nice but you didn't have body odour or not that anybody would notice anyway as you all smelt the same and it seemed to do the trick. I can only remember having the usual stuff like measles and chickenpox. Mumps I had when I was 23 and that was not a pleasant experience.

My early memories start at about four years old. Dad worked in the forestry commission and was a ganger (foreman.) A lot of the forests were being planted at that time and roads were being bulldozed all over the hillsides. At four years old Mum used to pack my piece bag with a flask and sandwich and I would set off on my own to meet Jack Salmon the bulldozer driver. He was a big man but gentle and he could move a lot of earth in one day making roads. I would meet him in the wood where we had parted company the day before and he never stopped talking all day. I even got to drive on an odd occasion when moving from one area to another. Of course that was the main attraction sitting in this enormous machine—driving it. He always waited and I spent nearly every day in the bulldozer with Jack until I had to go to school, which wasn't quite so much fun. In those days you were, even as a four year old, allowed to roam freely without the fear of being abducted or whatever, maybe folk had enough kids of their own to be bothered stealing somebody else's. I spent many happy days with the forestry workers. They had a workshop close to our house which was a short walk through the wood where I used to get my trike fixed. One day the engineer Jock Munroe welded my trike handlebars solid but Mum sorted him out—she didn't take fools lightly.

Chapter 2

Of course, eventually I had to go to school, which was about a three mile walk and in the company of my two brothers and one sister, all older than me, so my clothes and boots were on their third time starting school. My sister's probably weren't suitable, but I bet I wore some of hers, like jerkins and things, but not the blue knickers or

relaxing with friends

family photo smart jerkins

rare tie job Rob looks as uncomfortable as me

11

dresses. The only things we boys didn't share were underwear as it was worn out before it could be handed down. Boots were an option of course, mind you by the time I got them there were no toes left, or definitely nothing to polish. It was boots or bare feet—we didn't mind one way or another. We weren't the only kids at school in bare feet. There wasn't any competition for designer trainers, I don't think there was such a thing in 1955. Kids nowadays wouldn't wear the clothes we wore, especially hand me downs. The fashion was jerkins (a kind of zipping up knitted jacket) which all the kids wore and shorts which were almost to the knee and either corduroy or heavy checked cloth of some sort and thick knitted socks as seen in old photographs of our childhood. We didn't mind or know any better, and never complained about the distance to school either.

Possibly we were happier having to make our own entertainment. We spent most of our time playing in the newly planted woods. Sitka spruce was suddenly the tree to grow so there were thousands of acres planted in Glenlivet and surrounding areas. They grew straight and fast compared to other spruce species. We knew every path, burn, hill and shortcut through these woods, and never got lost and never gave Mum any reason to worry about us—she always had a good idea where we were.

Uncle Doug and Auntie Elle had moved to be our neighbours from a place at the other side of the woods called Tomachlowan, and later to a forestry cottage in Tomintoul where Doug was diagnosed with MS. It was a family disaster. Doug had to give up his work in the forests, which meant losing his house as well because it was a tied house. Their new house was in the town of Tomintoul, a council house, but it was all they could get, and at least it had a roof. They had two sons. When they were in Tomachlowan we used to walk across the hill about two miles to play with them. Auntie Elle, or Big Fat Ell as we used to call her as she was a bit big, was a very kind auntie and was always good to us and an auntie I kept in touch with for many years. Before moving to Glenlivet and marrying Elle, Doug had been a sign writer and a very good one, so he made his living for many years sign writing and did very well at it. Later when he had to give up they moved to Tomintoul and he lived the rest of his life in the council house where I used to visit and talk to Doug. Even although he couldn't talk back, he obviously enjoyed the company.

On one occasion we thought it would be fun to knock a bee's bike off a tree but that wasn't such a good idea because not only did the stings hurt, so did the thrashing we got for being so stupid. (Another school hazard was my cousins who lived up the road. One in particular, Chrissie, made me cry every day bullying me at school. Boy did I hate her.)

I also used to feel sorry for Martha, the school teacher's daughter, who was daily beaten by her mother in front of the class as an example and to show there were no favourites in her school. Funny in those days that teachers looked grumpy with a wrinkly old face, it must have been part of the training to look and live a miserable life.

On the way to school we had to pass the Inn where lived a really scary old woman called Miss Mackay. If we walked altogether it was ok but on your own it was run up the other side of the road and not even look. To be fair she did on occasion give us a drink of lemonade but we didn't hang about. Maybe she liked kids but we were having none of it.

At the back of the woods at Morinsh lived a family called the Mills, Sandy was normal, Beldi became my auntie but Henry was a bit odd. They were all tall people, six foot six plus, and built like tanks. Henry was the provider—at the end of the year salmon came up to spawn in the burn, but Henry had competition, otters. So he designed a trap—a funnel under a bridge, a snare and a 303 bullet. The bullet was fixed to the side of the bridge in a pipe. The snare was attached to a firing pin so that when the otter went into the snare it triggered the firing pin. We looked every time we passed but I don't think it ever worked. I wonder why, imagine now?

Sunday school was compulsory and it was 5 miles to walk. Sometimes Dad would take us to church and wait for us at Granny's. His then boss, known as Old Murray, took Sunday School. He'd tell us some stories and take us back to Granny's, where we would find Dad and Uncle Les and some other worthies playing pitch and toss behind the byre, pitch and toss being a gambling game which had been banned and was extremely illegal.

I didn't know my Granda Dingwall, he had died at the age of sixty four. He was opening up the cornfield, scything round the outside in preparation for the binder and he just dropped dead. I was only two. He had been a policeman before taking on the Shenval farm, which Uncle Les then took over. Les always grew his neeps (turnips) away at the back of the farm where there was a ruin, where he used to take us as a special treat. Some treat, we always ended up howing [hoeing] or pulling turnips. We always wondered why he kept his rifle and a stock of beasty ale, or beer, in the ruin until later we discovered why the neeps were grown so far from home but next to the forestry. It was to encourage the deer to come out of hiding in the woods so that they could have a constant supply of venison and anything else that moved—even an odd capercaille. Blue hare in the summer or white hare in the winter (it was amazing how they changed colour to suit the seasons) also came down from the hills when there was snow, so they were fair game as well. Hare soup was always something to look forward to. The blood from the hare was used as the stock and sometimes the front legs were added and then vegetables, and the rest was made into a stew. A grand feast indeed. The capercaille had to be buried for up to three months before you could eat it to get rid of the taste of resin. Since their main diet was pine needles the flesh had a very strong taste of resin, or so the story went. I never actually witnessed the digging up or the eating of the bird so can't say what it tasted like. It was obviously reserved for grown ups, or maybe never actually dug up again.

We could sit for hours listening to Les's stories. He always had a new story to tell. In fact in his later years when he retired he wrote and published some poetry.

I suppose Sunday School gave Mum a bit of peace for a few hours from four kids all born just over a year apart. I don't remember the cousins going, well they were from my dad's side of the family anyway and I don't remember any great communications between the two families. So Les's stories were more fun and we always called in at Granny's on the way.

Granny had what we called beasty ale, kept in lemonade bottles on the kitchen windowsill. It was some kind of yeast which grew and multiplied and you would transfer some into another bottle and start all over again. I think they drank it as a refreshing drink. Maybe it was alcoholic, it seemed to be a family secret and we were only allowed a small sip from Uncle Les when nobody was looking.

Uncle Les always called me Neil because he didn't like my name Nigel. Well neither did I very much, I don't know where Mum got that from, there weren't very many of us about, but I got used to it over the years. He never called me by my name as long as he lived, it was always Neil or Neilly, much to Mum's annoyance. But he was a favourite uncle and we loved going to the Shenval. He kept pigs and in those days you could buy broken biscuits from the factory as cheap pig food. Lots of them were chocolate digestives which we consumed almost till we were sick, never really having had much experience of chocolate—it was worth going to Sunday School.

Chapter 3

In 1956 we moved to live with Granda at the Downan, where he had a croft and where my dad had been brought up. After the first world war three of the soldiers returning to Glenlivet were given the tenancy of three crofts by the then factor of the Crown Estate as part of some resettlement scheme. Granda got one, the saddler got another and a man called MacPherson got the third one. Granda had all three crofts at one time but sadly gave up the other two before we moved in, but his own croft is still in the family and run by my sister to this day.

At some stage Granny had died, I don't remember her at all. I think I was about two but apparently she must have been a bit of an old grouch and was never really spoken about very much. Mum didn't like her, she ruled everybody. I suppose having had sixteen children would have had some effect on you.

I don't remember anything about the Downan prior to going to live there. Brother Bob remembers Granda having horses to work the croft but I only remember tractors—an old grey Fergie as it was known and Dad had it for many years. It did all the work on the croft.

I think we probably didn't visit much, well at least Mum and us didn't. Maybe it had something to do with Mum being pregnant at sixteen, pre marriage. O dear, we didn't actually know that till their 50th wedding anniversary came round and I don't know why, but somebody did a calculation and well, well, how did they manage to keep that a secret all that time? The rest of their families must have known, but kids in those days didn't get told about things like that. People dying was also considered a grown up thing. Uncles would disappear and aunties like Auntie Dot just seemed to disappear. They had a big family of cousins and suddenly they just stopped coming. Auntie Dot had died of cancer, and I don't remember seeing Uncle Sandy again.

Before all this we used to visit them and they used to visit us on a regular basis. Sandy worked on the railway and they lived on the Dava Moor on a small croft that was in the back of beyond, but was great fun for us because we got a run out in the old shooting-brake (a big car with a wooden back like an estate car.)

The first car I remember was an Austin 7—Dad's pride and joy. That is till the battery fell through the floor in Aberlour one day and Mum had to cradle it in her lap all the way home. But as the family grew year by year the Austin just couldn't cope and was traded in for the shooting-brake, although Dad struggled to keep it in petrol (it having a six cylinder engine.) It didn't pass many petrol pumps. We were taken to Oldmeldrum for twenty hens one time, one of Granda's deals with an old crony. Granda liked his hens and we were never short of eggs. When we had a clucking (broodie) hen I was given the task to cut a turf and put it into a small coup, make a small hollow in the middle and place a dozen eggs in the hollow and put the clucking hen in with the eggs. In twenty one days, with a bit of luck, you had a hatching of chickens.

Having collected the hens Dad got lost on the way home and ran out of petrol in the Caprach. It was dark. Not much chance of passing traffic in those days. So we slept in the car with the hens, which were loose, while Dad walked to Dufftown twenty miles away for petrol. It took him nearly all night so we settled down with the hens who didn't seem that bothered about us. I just remember waking up with a hen perched on my head, much to the hilarity of my siblings. Luckily, it didn't do anything more drastic while it was perched on my head and we did have fresh eggs for when we got home.

Even when Granda died several years later we were kept in the background and didn't know much about it even although we lived in the same house for many years and became very close. Even the women didn't go to the graveyard in those days, well not in Glenlivet anyway.

The Downan house was a stone house with 2 dormers upstairs but very small bedrooms and alongside it was a wooden, rat-infested sort of house. There was no electric so it was light on at 6.30 in winter—a tilly lamp powered by paraffin. You needed methylated spirits to heat up the mantle then you had to pump like mad to get pressure to supply the mantle with a continuous supply of paraffin. We had torches but very rarely turned them on because all you could see were little red eyes darting around the room. There were holes in the kitchen wall where the rats could come and go as they wanted. Granda's theory was that there was no point in filling the holes as they would just make another one. However Ma was having none of it. She had four kids and she didn't really want to move to the Downan from her fine new house to a rat infested dump where very little was hers and Granda was fairly set in his ways. But in those days women

Mum relaxing on the doorstep with Bob Lyn and Me

outside the old rat house with Auntie Janet

didn't have any choice and went with their man whether they liked it or not.

The rats got sorted and things got a bit better. I was never, and am still not yet, sure why Dad took over the family house and croft. There were eight acres of good land that went with the croft, but there were also sixteen children, two of whom had died at a very young age in the twenties. I never did find out how Dad was chosen as the lucky one. Ma certainly didn't think it was very lucky, her life was turned upside down and nothing was hers and she really didn't feel like it was her real home until Dad had the houses renovated in the early sixties. He knocked down the old wooden bit, I can't think of any other way to describe it, and extended the old house up the way to give more room upstairs. A contractor did the block work and the roof and Dad did the rest helped by yours truly (child slavery) and other members of the family who were in the trade, mainly Uncle Stan and Ally.

Dad bought two old prefabs from Buckie. There were hundreds to choose from, they had been built to rehouse home-coming troops and their families after the war. He then built one good one out of the two where the old wooden house had been and built concrete blocks round it and put a proper roof on it. From the outside you wouldn't have known it was a prefab.

Building it was like making a jigsaw—it was just a pile of bits and sections. The main frame was steel and the rest was all in sections, which eventually fitted together. The left over bits were used to build a hay shed and a garage for the car. It was a bit like when Uncle Willie came to sythe the corn, every night you came home from school you had to help, mixing cement or hold this or that (more child slavery) but it was good when it was finished, or nearly finished. I don't think it was ever finally finished but Mum could put her own touch to the house and make it feel like her home.

She went from looking after her four kids in a nice comfortable house (for those days) to looking after us, Granda and the livestock. In those days she had to milk the cow morning and night, feed the rest of the cows and stirks (young cattle), cream the milk, make the butter, and get us all off to school while Granda lay in bed and Dad went to work. Don't get me wrong, I loved my Granda but in hindsight he didn't just get his son back he also got a slave and early retirement.

After a few years Dad changed jobs and became the local postman (postie) as his dad had been before him. At that time it was all government run so his pension just carried on and that is what he did till he retired. He also ran a sweet van, or landrover, for the kids and helped old folks with their coal and sticks (more than he did at home.)

Dad with a rather snowie postie landrover

Granda used to 'do' the horses every day, as in bet on them. It seemed to be the only vice he had. It was only maybe three two-bob each way doubles every day and if he had a win he would allow you to pick a horse and put on a shilling each way. Of course you had to take his letter to the post office and buy the postal order which I did willingly as I found the selecting of the horses a daily excitement.

He used to let me play with his medals from the first world war, of which he had many. He had to live with a slightly disabled arm from the war when he was wounded in the Somme. A bullet had passed through his shoulder and damaged his ligaments so that he couldn't really open and shut his hand. Mind you it was a formidable weapon nonetheless and extremely strong and you didn't stand too close if you were in trouble.

Granda and I also played a lot of cribbage. You do your scoring on a wooden board with sixty one holes for each player, the object being to score multiples of fifteen and the first person round the board won. We spent many fun hours at that game. Of course Granda was an old cheat and would do anything to win, but I got better and wiser. I'm afraid it was a Grant trait, we were all bad losers and cheats and a lot of huffing went on over the years.

Unfortunately in nineteen sixty three Granda took a stroke and became partially immobilised and Mum had to look after him as well as all her outside chores, with very little help from Dad. She had to do it all herself even although it was HIS father and of course none of the other thirteen family members wanted to know, only posh Betty took him for a couple of weeks a couple of times. It was extremely unfair and it went on for five years until Granda demanded to be put in the peer hoose as he called it or as it was called in those days. The peer hoose ([poor house) was the name for an old folks home or hospital and the first time Mum went to visit he demanded his beets (boots) because he wanted home. But he stayed and spent the rest of his time in Dufftown hospital and died one and a half years later.

Mum and Granda and that's the party animal, Adie

Maybe that was why Dad was the chosen one—he didn't drink, didn't gamble and his days of chasing women were over when had to get married so young. I think all my uncles gambled and drank, some a bit and some a lot, most of them worked in distilleries.

Chapter 4

The school in Glenlivet was much bigger than Morinsh with three rooms and it was the same teachers all the time I was there.

school photo, cute eh?

The whole school in 1960

smart team in 1959

There was Miss Stuart, known as the Wee Missy, who was a young, (well we thought so anyway) teacher who taught the primary. She was always prim and proper, wasn't too grumpy, ran a wee Wolsley hornet car, didn't socialise very much and I think was a spinster all her life.

Now Miss Stewart, known as Stewpy, the middle room teacher, was a different kettle of fish. She ran an Allegra car which seemed to suite her, same shape and a bit contrary. She was older, stooped and a face that when she glowered you nearly wet yourself with fear. She used to throw things—anything—whatever was nearest, rulers, pencils, blackboard wiper which was wood with a cloth back. Failing that you got taken to the cloakroom where you got six minimum of the strap. Hers had four leather tongues and it did sting but it was more fun to watch her face as she raged and screamed at you with tears running down her cheeks. Her other special was to sneak up behind you and slap you on the ear with a ruler and that did sting and the surprise element normally had the desired effect and normally brought a very rare smile of satisfaction to her face. Some of the other boys used to tease her just to see how far they could push her and the primary seven boys used to hide her strap, which was okay as long as she didn't find out who it was. Everybody was interrogated, she must have been in the Gestapo, but there were no clypes in our room so everybody was given lines or some kind of punishment just for her own satisfaction. I never chanced it, I was too much of a wimp.

Of course she did have classes five, six and seven who pushed her to the limit. By the time I got to primary seven you had to pass the eleven plus to move up the ladder to go to high school at Aberlour or Keith. I'm afraid I and best pal Joe

class picture with the Dominie

Hendry didn't make the grade, we were the thick ones. Nobody seemed to bother, no lectures at home to do better, nothing, so they obviously thought we were thick as well. Poor Joe—well he just carried on as usual like me and as long as we could get a fag or a fag end we were happy enough. We were the first to sit the eleven plus.

My brothers and sister had already gone on to secondary and remained at Glenlivet secondary till they left. Most of the others who went to high school changed, especially the girls who seemed to go onto another level and didn't talk to us. Snooty bitches I think we used to call them. High school boys were far more interesting than us and the girls all seemed to change their voices and began to talk with a posh accent like the boys, making them fair game and we just couldn't resist the chance to pick on them, childish as it may have seemed. But we didn't think it was. They were always laden with a bag full of books and obviously thought they were superior, although their parents were no better than ours, farm workers and distillery workers who were mostly alcoholics.

It was interesting in later years when we had the cars and they needed a lift to a dance that the social difference disappeared and they came back down to our level and we all became good friends again. We were earning and they were at college with little or no money.

In those days we seemed to get a lot more snow so the playground was almost one large slide for a few weeks every winter. Nobody bothered about clearing it—there wasn't so much mollycoddling in those days. If you hurt yourself you were told to take more care but there was none of this running to the head complaining about poor wee Hamish hurting himself on the ice. I woke up once in the Wee Miss's room wondering where I was, having fallen on the slide and knocked myself out. Parents weren't called, you just got a drink and sent on your way with a warning. If your brothers or sister clyped when you got home your headache just got worse for being stupid.

Of course there was still Sunday School up to that stage. Mr Murray had retired and our new teacher was called Nobby Clark, an appropriate name—he was a clerk or something at the distillery and he was either bonkers or really religious, but he did give us a lift every Sunday which of course meant you couldn't jink, so maybe there was method in his madness.

It wasn't the same because he made you read the bible and sing and act. He was obsessed with doing plays but he also had quite a pretty daughter, not that that was any good to us as she was a bit of a snob and looked down on us mere peasants. Eventually we were good enough to put on a play in the public hall and I was a cute Felix the cat. He did also organise a Sunday School trip each year which involved going to Hopeman Beach (if you could call it that.) It must have been the filthiest beach in Britain, covered in soor (sewage.) You couldn't go in the water, but it was always a good day out. Lunch never varied either, you used to get big round tins of spam which were shared out along with crisps and jelly with flies in it, or so we thought. It was actually currants—it must have been a nutritional thing—it was delicious and I could still eat a good feed of spam and tattie crisps yet. Not so keen on the flee jelly though. We went in an old Willie Low's bus and we thought it was a long journey but in fact it was only about thirty miles. Mum came sometimes.

We also had a school trip, which was good fun, but to a better beach at Burghead. Again the spam and tattie crisps and flee jelly were served up for lunch. There wasn't so much freedom as the Dominie (Head Master) was there scowling if you stepped out of line.

Luckily Nobby got transferred for some miscalculations at work and I never saw him again, so that seemed to be the end of Sunday School. Anyway I must have done six or seven years altogether and by the time I was twelve years old it wasn't cool to go to Sunday School, and Joe never had to go. Where's the fairness in that?

Joe and I moved on to the top room as it was called, It was the Dominie (Heamaster's) room, for first, second, and third years. The Dom was never there and he would write instructions on the board and disappear for long periods. There weren't any more than eight pupils in the room when we were in third year. We were always first equal in the class, they couldn't decide who was the thickest. I don't remember getting class prizes, maybe Joe does. When we were in the first year there were more pupils because they had missed the eleven plus and had to stay to do the last three years. When you were fifteen of course you had to leave school and get a job.

It was always a mystery why the Dom came back smelling of pandrops mixed with something else, until you got promoted to garden duties and discovered his garage was full of empty Glenlivet malt whisky bottles, in fancy boxes, which meant it was the best of whisky. The penny dropped what the smell was. Not one or two bottles, dozens of them. I think in those days because he taught all the distillery children he qualified for a free supply of whisky. Of course you couldn't say anything because you wanted the privileges that went with third year (learning or not, as you were classed as thick, so you were treated as such.)

The Dom always called you by your last name. He obviously got frustrated teaching such a small number of pupils and every now and again he would have an outburst along the lines of,

'You lot are so thick and stupid without a brain cell between you I'm wasting my time trying to teach you.' Obviously a bad day or supplies had run out. Normally he was civil and pleasant.

By the time you got to third year you got all the privileges—sweeping up the fallen leaves for his compost heap, that went on for weeks. He liked his garden and so did Mrs Dom (never did know her name, she just didn't talk to us.) Then we had to dig the garden, it must have saved him a lot of grief from trying to teach us. 'We' was always Joe and I, and then we were free to have a fag when we liked. Other duties were to go to the canteen and help the cook, Jean. She was a nice person and I don't know if the Dom thought he was punishing us but we thoroughly enjoyed every minute of it—extra portions of good food especially jam roly-poly.

The food at our school was the best, Jean and Mrs Ingles, her assistant, were two really nice ladies and cooked the best of food, real food all made at the school. Not like the rubbish they get nowadays—not a chip in site.

We had three visiting teachers Mr Ferguson on a Tuesday, he taught years one, two and three, technical drawing in the morning and woodwork and metalwork in the afternoon. Rory MacDonald on a Thursday afternoon, he did gym. Mr Gray came on a Wednesday, he did art. The girls got a visiting female teacher on a Tuesday. Instead of wood work and metal work they got sewing and things—whatever else they might have taught girls, we weren't really very interested.

Mr Ferguson was a small, placid sort of man but very strict—he even brought the strap out now and again just to make sure nobody took advantage. My graphs and technical skills weren't really up to much in fact I didn't even get an exam paper when it came to the final year. He obviously knew it was a waste of time. But woodwork and metal work were far more interesting and I did reasonably well at that and still have coffee tables and letter racks to this day and nobody dare throw them out. I think the poker's lost. Davy Mackie was in trouble with Ferguson in the metal room when he was putting the twist in his poker and Ferguson demanded to inspect it so Davie handed him the hot end which resulted in screams of pain from both of them as Mr Ferguson got a bad burn and Davie got six of the strap. Tuesday was a day at school that most boys looked forward to and there were no girls involved, and it was something that was to be of advantage later when I took my trade apprenticeship. Mr Ferguson was extremely clever and as you got to third year he would talk to you about your future and give advice. It was probably as near as we got to a career officer as they either didn't exist or we weren't worth bothering about.

Rory was different. He was ex army and fit—I suppose he had to be, being a gym teacher. Boys and girls together was always a recipe for showing off, not that it did us any good, they still thought we were idiots, so there was always trouble and we never learned. The punishment dished out was a bit gruesome—6 skelps with the cricket bat on your backside or catch the medicine ball (a heavy exercise ball) 6 times. I think the bat was the preferred punishment at least it was quicker and then you had to stand in the corner looking at the wall for the rest of the afternoon. Of course you were supposed to be in shame but all you did was daydream or wonder where your next fag was coming from and be glad you didn't have to jump about all afternoon. Joe probably held the record for the bat punishment as he either wound up Rory by his lack of interest in exercise or Rory just didn't like him. But whatever, Rory had no mercy. After the first, second and third year numbers began to diminish gym suddenly stopped, or Rory did, and the Dom did it after that which was a bit more relaxed. You were mainly left to your own devices while he took refreshments.

Mr Gray the art teacher was everybody's friend. He was a brilliant artist and always brought out the best in you. Well not me, I had no artistic skills, but some others did. While we were all attempting our artistic skills Mr Gray sketched some of the pupils and produced some beautiful portraits which were treasured by the pupils lucky enough to be sketched. Mine still has priority on my walls and is still in the original frame. Again, as numbers dwindled, so did Mr Gray disappear.

Play times were always good fun, never any bullying or fighting, maybe an odd skirmish amongst the older boys but nothing that carried on to the next day. We were normally the best of friends. Rounders and football were the main games in the playground, or tag, and most kids joined in. There was no playground supervision, it just wasn't needed. Of course second and third year spent most of playtime in the loos smoking whatever we could get our hands on, mainly tabbies (left over cigarettes butts from grown-ups.) Joe's mum and dad and older brothers and sisters all smoked so it was easy for him to acquire fags without any detection and also his brothers gave him whole fags anyway. My mum smoked Woodbines, but not very many, and Dad didn't know (or she thought he didn't) and she used to, and still does, smoke up the chimney. So it wouldn't be very easy to steal one as she only bought them in tens. Of course Dad had a spell of smoking the pipe; it was all top secret apart from the puffs of smoke seen rising from behind the whin bushes when he would supposedly go to check the cows. It was a private joke between us and our mother because we used to watch him disappear behind a bush and wait for the smoke to rise, but we daren't say anything because he held very strong opinions about drink and smoke and swearing, and to mention even in jest would have had painful repercussions.

Getting to school and back was by bike, we had all sorts from basic bikes to racers but none of them were fit to be taken all the way to school. The authorities had started bicycle lessons and bike safety inspections so there was no way we could take our bikes right up to school as they didn't have a brake between them. We didn't need brakes, we just used our boots or wellies to stop, so we left the bikes in the wood at the bottom of the hill leading up to the school. Of course the person doing the safety and efficiency test couldn't understand why all the Grants passed their test when they didn't have any bicycles. We were experts at bike maintenance and bike control, you had to be with our bikes. We could probably have shown him a trick or two, like wheelies and off road skills which his townie pupils couldn't do. Of course we had been instructed by the Dom to bring our bikes to school, but there was no way we were bringing our wrecks near the school and he knew it. He probably got some amusement knowing that we had bikes and that we wouldn't take them to school.

He did sometimes take funny turns and decide to put on a play, a bit like Nobby, and you were all given a part to play. What this play was called I can't remember but I was the sailor, and was I cute! Proud parents came to watch. Well, Mum did

my earlier acting

anyway, as all her wee boys and wee girl were in it. When the Dom's room emptied there were no more plays as there was just a few of us left.

In the winter wellies were the most practical thing to wear at school but having to wear them all day in class was a bit hot and I normally got tormented with chilblains, which wasn't very comfortable. I used to run about in the snow in the evenings in bare feet then back into the house and dip them in hot water, which was supposed to be one of the cures. Burying bacon in the garden was another. I'm not sure if any of them worked to be truthful.

Leaving school seemed to come too quickly. In the secondary system we (myself and my pal Joe, that's all there was in the third year) had to sit our leaving certificate exam which involved in my case English and Arithmetic marked by the Education Board as main subjects and Maths, History, Science, Technical subjects, Home craft and Geography marked by the Dominie. I think we got an hour to each subject. The Dom would hand you your paper and hover about looking over your shoulder giving prompts and advice he shouldn't be giving, not actually giving you the answers but enough to make sure you got at least a G mark or even a G+. No numbers in those days, exam results were given as G-, G, G+ and VG. There was a lot of lecturing and revision before each session which must have made some difference. To give the Dom his due he did want you to get on and helped you as much as he could. The end result was I got a G+ in Arithmetic, a G+ in English, a G+ in History, a G in Geography, a G in Maths, a G– in Science, a nothing in Homecraft and a G in Technical drawings, not bad eh?

I got an interview at Aberdeen College thanks to him and my suspect exam certificate, although he did say before I went that he didn't hold out much hope for me, really encouraging. Up to that time my only claim to success at school was that I got a special prize book every year for perfect attendance, which I took great pride in collecting at the annual prize giving. If the Dom hadn't got me the interview at the college, which was a complete waste of time, and for which they kept half a day off my attendance, I would have had ten years perfect attendance. It was the only half day I had missed in all my time at school. Mum was not amused and told the Dom so, in no uncertain terms.

Chapter 5

So to the college interview and entrance exam I went. I think the interview went okay but the exam, which probably wasn't that hard, was a lot of general knowledge, like who was chancellor or who was your local MP. We didn't have TV until the early sixties, and I didn't read the newspapers except the racing pages with Granda. Even then the TV picture was a very poor BBC1 snowy picture. The aerial was on the top of a fir tree behind the house, and I mean the top—about sixty feet up. Uncles were summoned, ropes were run up the tree by the youngest, Ally (he was always game for a ploy) and the aerial was finally fixed to the top by a variety of brackets made by Ally, who was an engineer at a distillery in Dufftown. Of course that wasn't the end of it because it kept turning with the wind and Dad was constantly adjusting it.

Prior to our own TV we used to go next door to Mrs Maclean who had telly and didn't need an aerial on top of a tree. Every Saturday night at four o'clock we were allowed to go next door to watch Zorro for an hour. Mrs MacLean's house was very fancy and the furniture the same, so we had to sit down and not move for that hour in case we made a mess or got dirt on something. She was a very nice old lady and we always thought she was very rich, maybe because she had a TV before anyone else who lived around our area.

When TV got more popular Dad became obsessed with the insides of TVs and spent most of his spare time buying old TVs at salerooms, fixing them, and then lending them to other people, some never to be seen again. He also fixed other people's. If he couldn't fix it there was another telly nutcase in Elgin called Walter Ritchie who was a real telly engineer, supposedly, where he used to go with the ones that beat him. If that failed they went home to a shed. There was many a row in our house because when somebody came knocking at the door (no telephones in those days) to get their telly fixed, Dad would give them our telly till he fixed theirs, which was sometimes two or three days. Mum used to get really furious because then we didn't have a telly.

He just kept building sheds for storing old tellies. At one time we counted about forty. It was a bit of a family joke but he wouldn't part with them. In actual fact when the sheds were cleared and the tellies buried by a contractor who was working in the wood behind the house we buried sixty old TVs. The driver of the excavator was gobsmacked and had to make a bigger hole. Whoever digs them up will wonder what it was all about. We should have put an obituary in a box and put it in the hole explaining what the telly grave was all about.

Dad was a saleroom fanatic, he went to two sales every week. It was like a hobby. The house was furnished from salerooms (god forbid to buy something new) and every space in the sheds that didn't have a telly was full of junk. Mum is still using the top loading washing machine and spin dryer bought in the seventies at a sale room—that was an upgrade from the sixties twin tub.

My general knowledge was fairly limited. If they had asked me about poaching, fishing, shooting, sport or even playing cards I would have passed, but I didn't, so it was back to the career drawing board. Of course dyslexia was never heard of in those days, I was probably 6 or 7 or even older before I could read or write with any confidence. I remember the rows I got for being so stupid but I just couldn't string two words together. I could remember verbal instructions, although mental arithmetic was never a problem. I don't think any other member of the family had a problem—they were all pretty bright and did well at school. Dyslexia was to be recognised later in life in my own children.

Alison went to college to do secretarial studies and did very well, that was until she got pregnant, whoops! Well that was the promiscuous sixties for you. To say it didn't go down very well with the old man would be a bit of an understatement but again that's another story.

Bob had gone to Canada when he was ten years old to stay with Uncle Jim, who had started a joiners business in Lumphanan Aberdeenshire, where Dad had started an apprenticeship and learned his carpentry skills. Uncle Jim had then immigrated to Canada and started a very successful building business over there. We all trooped off to Aberdeen station to wave goodbye and Bob disappeared. We, and the rest of the kids, didn't make a big thing of it. Again I think it was one of those things we just weren't told about it, they certainly didn't ask our opinion

Bob off to Canada, cool haircut

anyway. In those days the adults were in control and you just went with the flow. The story that we were told in later years was that he went to keep their only son company and to eventually take over the business which the son wasn't interested in. I suspect there is more to it than that so I think I need to do a little more investigating and I might return to the mystery later. Bob returned two years later having got home sick. He returned to Glenlivet, finished school and started his apprenticeship as a mechanic at Elgin Central Engineers and at nineteen joined the RAF as an engineer and remained there for his twenty two years of service. He then went to work (and still does) for an agriculture machinery company on the East coast.

In the middle of all that Bob and I married twin sisters on the same day twenty third of March nineteen hundred and seventy one, I think. Anyway Bob is still with Elsie and they have three kids. In fact we all had three kids each first time round, some of us had a second shot at it and had another two, well, only me actually. My marriage only lasted eleven years. I might get back to that later as well.

Ian had led a similar life to me except he was a lot cleverer than me and didn't smoke at school, not that I can remember anyway. His cleverness showed in his skill to avoid punishment by climbing up a big beach tree behind the house and sitting on a branch defying Mum who he knew couldn't climb trees and who would stand at the bottom of the tree shouting at him to come down. But no way Ian was coming down, and she would eventually give up. He would sit there for hours till she cooled down, and when he did come down the punishment was never as bad as it could have been for whatever he had done. He left school at fifteen and went straight into the navy on HMS Ganges in Peterborough. It was what he had wanted to do for years. He was the only one who really knew what he wanted to do. I didn't have a clue. Dad didn't approve, nobody knew why. Probably something to do with the war and his own experiences in the troop ships going to North Africa and then fighting through North Africa and Italy with the eighth army as a Gordon Highlander, which is something I can't write about because he would never talk about it. As children we were interested but when asked about it but he just clammed up or changed the subject.

Bob and Ian all grown up

It was Mum and Granda who saw Ian off which must have been a bit daunting for Ian, having lived in Glenlivet and never being further from home than Oldmeldrum for hens when he was about twelve. But Ian proved Dad wrong and went on to have a very successful career, not only in the Royal Navy but also in the South African Navy, in communications. He married an English girl, Linda, or Big Linda as we know her (I don't know why as she's not big) who was also in the navy and they had three children. He retired from the Navy and Joined the Coastguards in Peterhead for several years then became a computer programmer until he retired in his fifties.

Alison, the oldest, had a more interesting life but I didn't have much to do with her as a child probably because she was four years older than me and saw me as a bit of a little pest. Well I didn't want to play with girls anyway, at least not in those days. She was very pretty and clever and left school and went to secretarial college in Elgin by bus every day. But her career was short lived when she became pregnant to Bernie who was from Glasgow. She had being going out with Bernie for some time, unknown to Dad, who, to put it mildly, didn't approve and didn't like him and tried everything to stop her seeing him. But she defied him and pregnancy was the end result, which was becoming common in the sixties. We liked Bernie, he was a bit of a role model, well to me anyway. He was quite small but sturdy and very fit and athletic, played football and was very good at it and in great demand. He was nicknamed Bernie the bolt, but always reminded me of Willie Henderson a Rangers winger from the sixties who was small but like a bullet on the field. He taught us a lot about football and I'm afraid poaching, drinking, shooting (which was normally more poaching) and fighting which we were never really into. In fact I've never had a fight in my life apart from school.

Bernie and Sis were jive experts, sometimes when they were in full swing the dance floor would clear to give them more room. They could have danced for the country if they had a mind to. Bernie always looked out for us at dances and in Glenlivet there used to be barn dances and you could be sure if there was a fight going on Bernie was in the middle or the cause of it and when his brother Paul came around they were unbeatable. It didn't matter how big they were 'the harder they'd fall' he used to always say. In the Glenlivet hall one time when there was a dance, a gang from Aberlour came just looking for trouble, and did they get it! They probably picked who they thought was the smallest person in the hall dancing, with the prettiest girl, and started pushing him around, and to give Bernie his due he very seldom started a fight because he wasn't a trouble maker. It was just that he was so small people picked on him and he took a lot of stick before he retaliated. But then he did and on this occasion brother Paul was in the hall. Ricky and his pals didn't know what hit them. They were sprawled across the hall floor before they knew it. Ricky and his pals never seemed to learn as we knew them quite well and they weren't fighters and always came off worst in a fight, of which they had many. Of course in those days half an hour after a fight they were all in a huddle, shaking hands and the best of mates sharing a drink.

But Bernie couldn't get rid of the pregnancy and Dad banished him from the house and Sis (as Alison was known to us, in fact Mum still calls her Sis, even although she's sixty seven) was gated. Dad was furious and there were daily rows in the house. It caused a lot of friction and of course as usual we, or at least I, didn't have a clue what was going on and was told nothing. But the rows continued. Sis defied him till he had to give in and agree to a wedding and accept the pregnancy, but he wasn't going to the wedding.

However he did in the end, and Sis and Bernie were married, and Michelle was born—or Mitch as she was called by everyone. Bernie was eventually allowed into the house and would you believe it the old man adored that bairn and couldn't do enough to help his new son-in-law and grandchild.

They lived in a distillery house on the back road as we called it and it was another place to visit to play cards and have a laugh—oh, and a fag. But they fell on hard times and Bernie got the sack from the distillery he worked at, I'm not sure why, but there was probably alcohol involved as he liked his booze. It meant they lost the house as well, although he was lucky and got another job in a distillery at Dalwhinnie. But that didn't last long either and they ended up in an old ruined house beside Cromdale and no work and by this time Johnny had arrived. Dad, having done a complete turnaround, helped as much as possible. I bet he was dying to say 'I told you so' but I don't know if he ever did. Bernie took to poaching again and eventually got caught with a boot load of salmon and got fined and his fishing gear and his old Ford popular confiscated. After that he worked on the same farm as me for a time. They then got a council house in Tomintoul where a local estate gave Bernie a job as a fishing gillie—they obviously thought it was better to know where he was, and he was helping paying guests to catch fish legally. He also did snaring and pest control using ferrets for the estate so he was in his element doing what he enjoyed, and of course there was a bigger graveyard so more worms to sell to his fishing guests.

Chapter 6

Of course there was more to life than school, thank god. I fished a lot—in fact every chance I got was spent on the Livet, the local river. I knew every pool and where you could get a trout almost anytime you wanted to, places where other people laughed at you, mocking that there was no way you could get a fish in that spot. Well I was the one with the trout. We had a theory that when you caught a trout from a particular pool it was automatically replaced, well it seemed like it because there was always another one the next time you went back. My fishing skills weren't very good, spinning and fly-fishing just wasn't on. I lived on a croft with an endless supply of worms, so that is what I used, although, mind you, you used to get worms in the dung midden but they had rings on them and we called them ring worms, not as in the disease ringworm they just had rings on them and I didn't like the look of them so I didn't use them and wouldn't even touch them.

My brother in law Bernie used to get his worms in the graveyard at night with a torch. He got lots of really big fat worms and used to sell them to the fishers on the river Avon and the Spey for so much a dozen and made a fair bit of pocket money. We never had the bottle to go to the graveyard, we had too much imagination and it was scary.

A number six hook weighed down with lead and baited with worms was my method—you used light coloured worms in the dark pools and dark ones in the light pools. My best ever fish caught by fair means was a four and a half pound sea trout, caught in the small pool just above what we called the swimming pool where we used to swim in the summer. Well I say swim—we were usually accompanied by tubes from the back wheel of the tractor—and I still can't swim yet, fifty years later.

The fish was beautiful. It must have just run from the sea as it still had sea lice. I was with Joe and two other pals, the Meldrum boys, which is just as well because nobody would have believed me. I was a proud thirteen year old walking home that night carrying my first big fish and Mum was real proud of me. As there was too much for us the fish was divided up and shared with the other boys' families. It was the proudest day of my life. It was possibly the only legal big fish I ever caught as it was very rare to get an early run of sea trout that far up the river in the early summer. The Livet was a tributary of the river Avon which in turn was a tributary of the river Spey. It was into August and September before you got the salmon and sea trout going that far up, which they did in their thousands.

There was a family called Stuart who lived in the village of Bridgend, so named because it had an old, possibly a Telford, bridge which had two humps, at the end of the village. The Stuarts lived in the end house in front of the bridge. Under the bridge were big slabs which were probably the base stones and under the big flat stone lay the fish. The father, Old Charlie who walked with a bad limp (probably from the war) was the local gravedigger (I wonder if he got his worms from the graveyard?) He was also the local hall keeper. He used to let us into the hall after a dance or whatever had been on in the hall to collect the tabbies but we didn't pick up the ones with lipstick because normally the lipstick had soaked through the paper and discoloured the tobacco and we drew the line at that. We would then take the tobacco and roll it in fresh papers with a tip in it which you could buy in the shop for next to nothing. He had three sons and I think two daughters. Paul, who was probably three or four years older than me, lived at home and worked on a local farm as a general farm worker. He did smoke, Bristol, but didn't drink, not like his dad who really liked a good dram. Paul always had a good motor bike. While, when I got to sixteen I had a Vespa or Lambreta scooter for a tenner, Pauli (as we called him) had a Velocette motor bike—a very fancy bike which was all covered in and really shone. It also had a gear stick which was a bit odd.

The Stuarts knew every fish that went up the river since the fish had to pass under the bridge where they used to rest (that's the fish of course) having just negotiated a rather nasty falls in the river and were just about to come to another. If they stopped too long it was the end of their journey.

Not only did Paul have a good motor bike he had the best of fishing gear, a rod for every occasion and several reels. He was an expert fisherman, taught by his father. He could spin, use fly, use worms and most of all he quite often used no bait at all and still managed to catch fish. He had the polaroid glasses that could see fish in the dark water.

Most nights in August and September were spent fishing. I remember having spent a whole night fishing and getting nothing while Paul had half a dozen lying on the bank and he took pity on me and gave me a five pound grilse which I took home and lied to my mum and younger sister Lyn that I had caught by myself and I bribed Lyn with a Bar Six not to tell. I didn't catch very many but Paul had the ripping method off to a tee and he caught loads. He always had two rods with him, his heavy rod which he used for poaching and a fancy fly rod which he kept close by so that when the water baillie came sneaking around he just threw his big rod into the long grass and started fishing with the fly rod.

We had a few close shaves with the baillies. One time there was a big spate of water and we were in one of our favourite pools close to the main road. Paul had five or six salmon hidden in the long grass when the baillie suddenly appeared at the other side of the river. He didn't have time to change rods so he just left his line in the water as if he was worm fishing. The conversation went something like this.

'Hello lads, how's the fishing going tonight?'

'Aye not bad Baillie, not much doing just trying a bit of worm fishing the night as there's too much water for the flies.'

Of course he knew, and we knew, he couldn't get across the river because it was too deep. But he knew we had fish, and we knew that he knew, but there was absolutely nothing he could do so he eventually said,

'Oh well lads, good luck! I better get going and if you leave that worm in the water much longer it will be drowned.'

We weren't long before we headed for home and he found a way round to our side of the water.

Of course they knew we were taking fish but we were probably the small fry and not worth bothering about, but we weren't taking any chances.

I'm not sure what Paul did with all the fish but I assume he sold them to the game dealer in Cromdale who's name, by the way, was Slaughter, which we always found a bit funny. But sometimes you just get people whose names suit their occupation. In those days he would and could buy anything he wanted from anybody. He did always ask where you got whatever you brought in but you just lied. Maybe that was why Paul always had good kit.

Paul was a good friend and we used to go shooting with his car. Pheasants or roe deer were fair game, which were always passed on to Mr Slaughter. His car was an Austin 7, a bonny car and he was proud of it. It sparkled with attention. That is until we were away out of our territory one day at Ballindalloch where we knew the estate reared pheasants and we were guaranteed a pheasant or two. Having bagged one bird, I was the runner. Paul fired the shot and I ran to pick up the victim and jumped back into the car and off we shot down the road. Of course we always kept the gun, a side by side dog hammered twelve bore shotgun, in between the seats and as I jumped back into the car I bumped the gun which in turn caught one of the hammers on the side of the seat and pulled it back and when I made a grab for it, it went off and blew a hole through the roof of the car. The roof of the Austin 7 was made of canvas kind of stuff so it made a big hole, but it also meant it was repairable. We just sat and stared at each other for a minute or two until we realised what had happened. Paul was gutted. His bonny car wasn't so bonny now with a big gaping hole in the roof—even writing this now has my adrenaline running at speed. I think it was one of the biggest frights of my life. Needless to say we never kept a loaded gun in the car again and the wee Austin, which never looked the same again, was soon traded for a classy Hillman Minx, which meant that when we went to get a pheasant someone sat in the back holding the gun unloaded. We didn't class the pheasant shooting as poaching because it was always for the pot and never ever encountered a gamekeeper on our expeditions. They obviously turned a blind eye knowing it was for the pot, well in my case anyway.

Paul's brother Charles was in the navy so when he came home we were never short of fags as he had thousands of duty free fags he got while posted overseas, or so he said. Rothmans King Size they were and he was very generous with then too. While Charles was at home we didn't go without, no picking up tabbies, it was the real thing and big ones at that. On a Saturday afternoon I would go up to my Uncle Eddy and Auntie Elsie's house where they had good telly and watch the wrestling and have my tea—usually chips and burger with beans. The wrestling was always good fun. Auntie Elsie was Glaswegian and got really up tight when the match wasn't going her way and nobody argued with her or you were liable to end up in a submission hold and when it finished she returned to her placid old self—a good laugh and one of my favourite aunties.

Usually after tea in the months of August and September when he wasn't on shift, Eddy who worked at the distillery, would take me fishing—his style. No rod was involved in this operation just a snare on a two to three foot stick carried down the leg of his trousers, a gamekeeper's bag and polaroid glasses. We would walk up the river for about two miles where there were long pools and overhanging banks where Eddy would proceed to look over the edge and under the bank till he found the appropriate victim lying in the best position. The snare was then slid over the tail with great expertise and in a flash the fish was on the bank. He never missed once in all the times I went with him. Again he caught for his own use or to orders from local people, never to sell. He tried to teach me the art but got fed up of me missing or touching the fish with the snare so my apprenticeship didn't last long and I was relegated to look out duties again—that is look out for the water bailiffs.

Eddy also liked a bit of venison and now and again he would come to our house on the edge of the wood, which in turn led onto the open hill where there was an abundance of roe deer. There were always two guns in our house which Mum kept locked away. They seemed to be available to the brothers if they wanted, but they had to get them from Mum first. She didn't like guns and she didn't like poaching, which they were doing the minute they stepped over the fence at the back of the house. The two guns were a twelve-bore shotgun and a .22 rifle. The .22 was always used for the deer but it wasn't that easy. Roe deer are very nervous creatures and some days you would go for hours and get nothing. I don't think we shot that many but if we got lucky Eddy would hang them up in the back shed for a few days. Mum hated it and couldn't wait for him to come back and chop them up and take them away, refusing offers of free meat as she wanted nothing to do with it.

Of course Eddy was great in our eyes—he always took us shooting and could do no wrong and we didn't get involved in the arguments about the guns. He also used to get the pheasants from the corn stacks by soaking barley in bullins—the dregs from empty whisky barrels obtained at night by going through the supposed empty whisky barrels and tipping them up into a bucket and collecting any liquid that was in them. Some of it was good, if they got a good sherry cask but mostly it was rubbish, although some of the distillery workers who got desperate and couldn't get whisky anywhere else would drink it and I imagine spent a lot of time in the loo and with really bad hangovers as it was pretty potent stuff. He would then scatter the mixture around the corn stacks, go back the next morning and pick up the best pheasants that were lying about intoxicated and leave the rest to sober up. He never killed hen pheasants and only took cock pheasants, maintaining there were too many cocks in proportion to hens! Uncle Ally was probably the most frequent user of the guns which Mum used to lock up and if anybody wanted to use them they nearly had to wrestle her for them because she hated having them in the house and didn't like anybody using them. I wasn't allowed until I left school, spoil sport.

Ally was the youngest of the brothers and married late. When he was single he would turn up most weekends to help on the croft and do some shooting, mainly roe deer, pigeon and pheasants and often he would take us to the dunes, a raised area claimed to be the site of a battle in the old days. There were always rabbits and hares so very exciting for us as teenagers to be taken on these expeditions. The same area was also a good breeding place for lapwings and oystercatchers so in the spring when Ally came we would go and collect their eggs but we always had to leave one egg in each nest. We would then take them home and test them in a basin of water and if they floated we didn't eat them, the rest were boiled and shared out as a treat. They were very rich and tasted better than any hen egg.

In the early sixties there were hundreds of ground nesting birds, now you hardly see any, maybe because we ate all the eggs. He also came home with a capercaille, and buried it, but again I never saw the end result so I still don't know what they taste like—maybe it's still there.

He also didn't like cats and we had a tabby cat who was known as Ma mainly because she was always having kittens which Ally was more than willing to dispose of. On one occasion we were to be allowed to keep a kitten and were asked which one we liked best so we chose a bonny black and white one. But Ally, whose sense of humour was much to be desired, kept the ugliest ginger kitten which had us all howling, much to his amusement and mother's rage, so he wasn't very popular then either. Maybe if we had asked for the ginger cat to be kept he would have kept the black and white one. I still cast it up to him now having found out he has a cat that he adores and takes for walks every day! At one time, unknown to anybody, he tried to dispose of Ma by putting her in a sack with some stones for weight and threw her in the river, but by the time he walked backed to the house Ma was sitting at the door. She was back before him, having clawed through the sack we assumed. Mother was furious when she found out and Ally was told in no uncertain terms he wouldn't be welcome if he tried any more of those antics. He then proceeded to shoot any tomcat he could see which was more welcome as it meant Ma had fewer kittens and the cattle feed didn't stink of cat pee. We later found out that Ma didn't actually reach the river and Ally took cold feet and let her go and just threw the empty sack in the water, the big pussy cat.

In general he was good fun to be around and was well liked by us all, surprisingly enough. Every year while Granda was alive all the brothers would come and clean the ditches in the peat moss and cut peats for the croft. Even Walter, who was Managing Director (or something big) in the Scottish Malt Distillers at the time would get the waders on and get covered in peat which didn't smell very good. I bet his wife Betty didn't let him in to the house till he was clean as she was a bit of a snob and thought herself better than the rest and her house was always perfect. They had two children. Allan was a bit of a clever clogs. He was very clever but Shirley was okay.

Chapter 7

Although holidays were very rare in our house I did have one or two and one summer I was sent to Walter and Betty's to play with Allan and Shirley—that is, after a shopping trip to upgrade my wardrobe. It was a waste of time and money as it was probably the worst holiday ever—strict rules and not allowed to play with other kids. Even worse there was a strict bathing and washing regime. I was never so clean in my life and probably never been so clean since—I think Mother struggled to recognise me when I came home. Allan and I had nothing in common and I didn't play with girls, well not then anyway, and I was always in trouble. I'm sure Allan did some of the things I got blamed for and I, being a bit thick, didn't realise what he was doing. Anyway I was used to getting the blame. At home when something went wrong Dad would ask Bob,

'Was that you?' Of course Bob said,

'No, it was Ian,' who would say,

'No, it was Nig,' (as I was known) and I got the clip round the side of the head without even being asked. Of course the other two had a satisfying smirk on their face knowing I had got the blame again. So I never got another holiday at Walter and Betty's.

I had one other holiday, at Uncle Donald's and Auntie Ruby's. They had moved in beside us at Morinsh when Dougie and Ellie left, and Donald worked with Dad. I was always a favourite with Ruby,

47

she thought I was cute (how people change their minds!) Donald after a while moved to be the head gardener at Crathie Castle in Aberdeenshire. Ruby had a nephew called Raymond and I was sent to keep him company in the summer holidays. Raymond was a right little twerp. He was an only child and spoiled rotten and obviously resented me being there. But to Ruby who was very prim and proper. He was her blue-eyed boy and could do no wrong and he knew it. Donald and Ruby never seemed a very good match because Donald was a very good gardener and was fairly down to earth and set in his ways, and liked a drop of whisky every now and again. Ruby, on the other hand, liked everything to be perfect and tidy and couldn't abide alcohol. Donald used to keep half bottles hidden around the garden and when I caught him scooping one day I was sworn to secrecy. Luckily his creepy nephew wasn't there as he would have grassed him up to Ruby so it was our secret. But Ruby was no fool and when he'd had a few swigs she could tell by the permanent grin on his face. We would then be sent from the room and Donald would get interrogated as to where he got the booze and ticked of accordingly, but he just sat there with a big grin and took it all on the chin.

It wasn't much of a holiday as Raymond didn't like me, but the feeling was mutual. I was in trouble on a daily basis and Ruby must have thought I was a troublemaker (I went out of favour very quickly and my cuteness went out the window even quicker) but half the time I didn't know what I was in trouble for.

The estate had free-range hens which was a big attraction to me as I loved my hens at home. I was allowed to help feed them and collect the eggs, but almost on a daily basis there would be a piece of fence pulled up allowing the hens even more free range and there's nothing worse than trying to herd hens as they are pretty stupid when it comes to common sense and directional skills. Well pigs are just about as bad but at least you can get to grips with them. I got blamed every time—it couldn't possibly be the golden boy as he never ever did anything wrong but he always knew because it was him who ran clyping to Ruby. It didn't matter how often I protested it made no difference. If she had just looked at the satisfied grin on her blue eyed boy's face she would have known the truth, so the friction grew and eventually I gave him a hiding which in turn resulted in me being sent home in disgrace as it couldn't have been poor wee Raymond's fault. Of course Dad wasn't very sympathetic either because he had to drive all the way to Crathie to pick me up, neither Donald nor Ruby drove and never did. The up side was I was never invited again to Donald and Ruby's for the summer holidays, thank god, and I don't think I ever saw Raymond again. Come to think about it I never got invited anywhere again for my summer holidays. It must have got round the family that I was nothing but trouble. Anyway it was better fun at home.

Donald then moved to be head gardener at Poolewe gardens on the West of Scotland, and was there for many years till he retired. I didn't see him again for about 50 years.

The Grant family, Granda and all the sons, played bridge—a stupid card game that I could never understand—and they took it very seriously. They played every chance they got. You needed four players but if they didn't have four players they would play a dummy, as in an invisible person, just so that they could play. When Donald stayed beside us at Morinsh Ruby wouldn't let him out, especially to play cards. Ruby was from the city and was used to getting a lot of attention. Dad and Donald were known to get caught playing bridge over the garden fence with two dummies. They all took it very seriously and even had their own bridge club and league in the local hall where they met up on a Thursday night. Dad had made a big wooden box where they kept their tables and cards locked up so that nobody could use them. It was almost as bad as the freemason sect.

We did play cards but it was nine-card brag, which we played every Sunday night at home. Mum played. So did Granda, our pals Joe and his brother Rob, Paul the poacher, Andrew Meldrum, Gordon Forbes, Davy Mackie, brothers and sisters. We all played—for halfpenny stakes and if the kitty wasn't won that Sunday it was carried forward to the next. At one time it got to one pound, which is a lot of half pennies but well worth playing for (it could have been worth a packet of fags.) Paul won it, the git, the tension was that bad that even Mother got ratty.

Uncle Gordon was the black sheep of the family and was never made welcome at home. Dad wouldn't talk to him although it had been his home, where he was born. He would come to visit two or three times a year. I don't think he ever visited any of his other brothers or sisters—it must have been something that happened in the family years before. He had a bad drink problem but there was never any evidence when he visited. He worked on farms around Elgin in Morayshire till he accumulated some money. They said when he had money he had plenty of friends or hangers-on, as I would call them, till all the money was gone and no friends when he was broke. We liked him. Of course at that time we didn't know the history, we looked forward to his visits as he nearly always brought us something like a pet rabbit or a guinea pig or even just sweets. He was full of stories—where he'd been and what he had been doing. Maybe he made them up but we didn't care we enjoyed sitting in a group listening to him. Mum liked him too and would feed him, unknown to Dad as that would have been trouble. Granda was always good to him as well and I'm sure gave him money when he left. After Granda died we never saw or heard of Gordon again until he died several years ago seemingly having settled with someone in Elgin, hopefully having some pleasure after all.

Chapter 8

Charlie Michie was the forestry commission gamekeeper, or ranger as they are called now, and he used to take me on his rounds. He cycled everywhere carrying his gun and game bag. It was mostly vermin control—rabbits, pigeons and deer. I was never taken on the deer outings but went quite a lot with him to the rabbits and pigeon shoots. Pigeons were a big problem. Farmers grew a lot of turnips for cattle and sheep feed and the pigeons would destroy a field of young turnip plants in no time. So we would sit behind the dykes and wait. They always came in flocks for some reason or another and Charlie would shoot forty or fifty in an hour. It was at one of these sessions that I got to fire my first shot with a twelve bore shotgun. I didn't take much persuasion to give it a go, in fact none. I couldn't wait! First he emptied a cartridge of the wads and the powder and put it in the gun and gave it to me with a long lecture about guns and the dangers and all the safety rules which I listened to and I never forgot. So the cartridge was loaded into the gun and I was given more instructions then the big moment BANG—and nothing—there was no kick, which I had expected because when Charlie fired the gun he always jerked back. So he then put a loaded cartridge in the gun and handed it to me and warned me that this would be very different and told me to brace myself. I fired the gun and thought my shoulder and chin had exploded. I landed on my arse on the ground and I wasn't that sure about the pants. All I could hear was Charlie's laughter through my dirling ears. It made his day! His only concern was his gun. It got easier with every shot after that until I became a fairly good shot. That was the beginning of my shooting exploits and I spent many evenings with Charlie behind a dyke hoping for another shot, which I got on a regular basis.

Although I spent many enjoyable evenings and weekends playing or shooting with my mates we always had to do our chores on the croft first. In the morning I had to muck out the byre. There were only 4 cows but they still produced two or three barrowfuls of dung morning and night which you then had to push up a plank to the back of the midden and tip it out. Not easy when you are only ten. You then had to hash the neeps which was done in a manual machine that you put the neep into and pulled down the handle which forced it through some blades leaving slices which fell into a scull and were then carried to the cows who were tethered two to a stall. You had then to manoeuvre yourself between two cows, who of course were getting desperate by this time and would sometimes kick at you or squeeze you between them while you pushed towards the trough. Their other trick was to try and get as big a share of the neeps as they could by butting the scull when you tried to share it out. The worst cow was called Adie, after Auntie Adie who was a very quiet person, a nice person, unlike the greedy awkward cow that was named after her. That is until she went to a wedding where, after a gin or two, Adie became a different person, dancing, singing not only on the floor but also on the tables—a bit like on 'You've been framed.' Next day it was back to the very quiet Adie (or a very embarrassed Adie) as she was told of her out of character antics.

For the calves or younger stock you had to cut the slices of neep into fingers in case they choked and of course Mum milked the cow, who in those days was called Morag. Morag produced the best of milk which was nice to drink warm straight from the cow. It was then poured into basins till the cream settled on the top. The cream was then skimmed to put on the porridge, but most of it was made into butter and the whey (the liquid that is left after the butter) was turned into crowdie, which could be spread on oatcakes. All the cows had names, usually after aunties and any male calves after uncles. When the calves were big enough and separated from their mothers they were moved to another shed about one hundred yards up the road in front of Mrs MacLean's house. We then had to carry food over to them as Dad kept them till they were over a year old. Of course they weren't tethered so they needed to be bedded with straw every day. There was one particular stirk (young cow) called Stanley who was a bit bonkers and when you went to do the bedding he would career about kicking his heels in the air and bellowing so we were banned from going in beside him and Dad had to do that bit himself. When it came to selling Stanley and his mates it took a lot of gates and men to get him into the lorry and Stanley became a legend never to be forgotten.

The calves were all clipped (as in having their hair cut to make them look good before they went to market.) The cattle man at Minmore farm used to come. Old Archie as we knew him was a very small man, never seen without a bonnet and didn't smile a lot and took life and his job very seriously. He seemed to think he was the only person given the gift of clipping

Ian and I training the calves for the halter

cattle, which involved clipping their heads as far back to just behind the heads and their tails just over the tail head, the idea being to make the head look smaller which in turn made the rest of the body look bigger and clipping the tail made the back look straight and even. Old

Archie, to be fair, clipped a lot of other cattle for farmers especially for taking to the shows where there were a lot of critics. If you did not, god forbid, ask Archie to do your cattle he went in to a big, big huff, as happened one year when he couldn't come at the right time and Dad got Brookie, the blacksmith, to come who was just as skilled. The next year when asked if he would come Archie would make some sarcastic comment like,

'Why don't you get Brookie to do it? He was good enough last year.' But he always came. We hated the job, which in those days, like everything else (well on our croft anyway) involved child labour. The clipping machine was manual and involved turning a handle to drive the clippers and if you didn't turn it at the right speed you got caught up in another kind of clipping which involved your ear.

Brookie had a farm neighbouring with us and we used to help him. He was a good farmer and had won most of the shows with his livestock. He always had a good yin, or two every year and I sometimes helped in his byres where he used to feed an enormous amount of feed, which he mixed himself. Nobody else was told the recipe but it involved a lot of something called bran. I was never allowed to see what he fed them, but it obviously cost him a lot to be up at the top. He was also, well, not lazy, but had a way of getting you to do all the work which I didn't mind at the time, but it was the promise of payment that got to me and Mum, who really got annoyed by the same promise every time of, 'I've nay money in ma pocket the day but I'll see ye the mora.' And that's what he said every time but the mora never came. Even years later I used to say to him sort of half joking, 'You haven't paid me yet Jock.' But he just laughed. He was the worst tractor driver I have ever seen. He had a MF135 Tractor but he was always in a snoral (muddle) of some sort, maybe to do with him being as blind as a bat. He wore glasses with really thick lenses, and in his younger days enjoyed a whisky or two, aye and sometimes three or four when he went to do some work at the distillery.

Despite all that he was a first class blacksmith and was one of the last smithies to shoe horses in the area. He also had top class bulls and because we only had three or four cows Brookie would bring his bull round to put our cows in calf, which was another performance. If the cow was too big we then had to dig a hole in the ground, on a slight hill if possible to back the cow into so that the bull could do his business and depending on whether you wanted a bull or heifer calf Brookie's bonnet would be positioned to suite. If you wanted to get a bull calf he would turn his bonnet backwards on his head. Although it sounds a bit bonkers it was part of the performance and we really believed it would work.

Most weekends we had the weekly chores on a Saturday—we thrashed corn for the week's supply of straw and oats, and we pulled enough turnips for the week as well to keep the cattle fed. Thrashing was boring for me. Being the smallest I had the job of tramping the straw and bagging the corn. Bringing the sheaves of corn in for thrashing was always fun because it was stored in big stacks built outside. They had to be built properly so that the rain would run off rather than into the stack and didn't soak them, so Granda built the stacks till he wasn't fit anymore then old Willie, the farm grieve at Drumin Farm, came along to do it, having been taught the art as a teenager. Nobody else was allowed to touch, especially the top, which had to be shaped to perfection. The corn was stooked in the field after being cut with a binder, which had been preceded by great Uncle Willie and his scythe.

Every year in September Uncle Willie and Auntie Anne would come for three weeks holiday, not by invitation because Mum dreaded them coming, but they came every year anyway and Willie would rod (cut round the edge ready for the binder) the corn and Anne would sit about like a big slug (that's probably a bit unfair.) But she was big and always claimed to eat healthily. Didn't we know it! We were made to eat peas meal brose every morning which was a brown kind of meal which looked like it had just been delivered by a very sick calf, and we had to sit and take forty chews to every mouthful of food, even the brose. I don't know what her diet must have been at home if that is what healthy eating does to you. We didn't want to know, she was not our favourite auntie. Apparently they lived in a very rough block of flats in Paisley—we seemed to have a lot of relations in Paisley. We're not a very good family at keeping up with relations, not like some, so maybe it was their annual escape to civilisation, but we didn't know that at the time. Anyway, Willie would proceed to rod the corn and after school, before we got fed, we were sent to gather the corn into bundles and make bands out of corn and tie the bundles into sheaves, gather them into eights and stook them. It was hard, tiresome work, or so

old aunties and an uncle with Dad and Granda

we thought anyway, and child slavery comes to mind, so apart from having to do the corn we stayed well clear of the pair of them and Mum used to give a big sigh of relief when they left.

When we went to take in the corn for thrashing we used to put a short piece of netting round the bottom of the stacks to stop the rats running away and we would kill them with grapes and bits of sticks and, of course, Joe the cairn terrier who could kill a rat with the shake of his head. The most rats in one stack was fifty four. The out-pouring would start very slowly but the further down the stack more and more would start to make a break for it, only to be met by the netting and no escape. That was the idea of the short net—you could kill the rats as they tried to get out of the net and any that did Joe would dispose of. Then when you got to the last few sheaves Joe was sent in to finish off the rest which he did with great pleasure, although he did come out with a few nose bites and you would hear a few yelps now and again. On one occasion I managed to grab a rat and try to kill it with my pocket-knife but it tried to chew my finger off so I quickly dropped it with a scream and Joe did the rest as I nursed a very sore finger. It didn't kill me and a lesson was learned—don't pick up live rats as they might bite and their skin is very thick.

That was like the squirrel I saw one time trying to struggle through the deep snow. So my way of it was I would pick it up and put it up a tree but the little shit bit a chunk off the point of my finger so it quickly landed back in a snow drift and eventually made its way on its own to the nearest tree—that's gratitude for you!

The thrashing always took place on a Saturday. We all had a role to play and mine was always tramping the straw, maybe because I was the smallest or the most useless. It was certainly the dirtiest job. Then the corn had to be bruised—you can't feed whole corn to cattle as they can't digest it properly. The bruiser was very old and we had got it from the old corn mill at Teetabooty when it was decommissioned. Dad and I were bruising one evening and the bruiser exploded throwing us both out of the shed. It was in a thousand bits and slithers of steel were stuck in the wall and some through the wooden door. How we didn't get killed I will never know, but Dad got a big scare and the first thing he said was 'Are you okay, Nigel?' Was that a real sign of affection? It made my day as the explosion was no big deal and I soon got over it. Needless to say I was never allowed near the new bruiser, Mum saw to that. I think I was a bit of a mammy's pet really.

Most tasks on the croft were ofetn easier in winter when it was cold and frosty. That is except neeps, which had to be pulled every weekend otherwise they went rotten, or that was what we were told anyway. This involved using a pickaxe to dig them out of the ground.

One person would go ahead picking out the turnips and the other trying to top and tail them with a tool called a tailer, which was a steel blade with wooden handle at one end and a hook on the other end to pick up the neeps. It was called a tailer for obvious reason. Whoever designed it should have been drowned at birth because it was quite a deadly weapon and you had to watch your fingers because they were normally that cold you wouldn't have noticed if you chopped one off. It was also used to knock off the big lump of earth that was frozen to neeps. Normally you would put four drills into one for easy loading into the trailer. Digging then could be fairly warm work once you got going, but loading them into the trailer out of a foot of snow was not much fun as the snow stuck to them and made life more difficult. You felt like your fingers would fall off, if you could feel them at all that is. In really bad frost we had to use a pick-axe to dig the neeps out of the ground.

Of course planting the neeps was a bit of a palaver as well. The drills for the neeps had to be dead straight and again it was a neighbour who did the drilling because he was the best straight driller. On more than one occasion I saw the whole acre of drills flattened and drilled again straighter. There seemed to be a lot of critics about, driving slowly down the road checking the drills, and not only ours. It was obviously some sort of competition. It's what farmers do well—talk about and criticise other farmers. If only they could have seen my drills on Colonsay in my attempts to grow neeps—they would have had a lot to talk about.

at the hoeing with Uncle Walter

must have been Xmas

firewood fun

Dad also seemed to pick the coldest day in the winter to dress and pick the tatties (potatoes.) It was one of those jobs you never forgot—sitting in the middle of a field at the tattie pit, picking the sprouts off the tatties and separating the seed from the eating ones and throwing out the rotten ones. The hay was cut in June or July with the old Fergie tractor and a finger mower, which took about two days to do two acres because of the mole heaps clogging up the blades. It was then turned by tossing it over with pitch forks (more child labour) twice a day for several days till it was dry enough to be raked into rows with a big wide rake towed behind the tractor and operated by a person sitting on it. When instructed you pulled the handle to release the hay ready to put into hoiks which were small heaps of hay. After a further few days, depending on the rain, they would be lifted by a hay lifter, which was like a big buck-rake, and taken to be built into haystacks which were supported by tripods (three poles set like a wigwam and held together by wire.) The hay was then left for a few weeks to make sure it wasn't heating and then transported by trailer to the hayloft above the byre ready for the winter. Hay was very labour intensive but it was a good fun time because there were always other people about to help and the weather was warm. Normally after a day at the hay we (me and my brothers and sister) would go to the pool at the bottom of the fields and play in the river to cool off.

The other feed we had for our cows was draff, which was a by-product of the distillery. It's the left over barley once they have taken out all the goodness to make whisky. We got a cart load every week and it wasn't unknown for us three boys to be balancing on the mudguards of the wee Fergie tractor going the three miles to the distillery for our weekly quota. The loading hopper would hold a whole mash which was about twenty five tons and our converted horse cart

me and the old Fergie

held about one ton, so it was a very precarious operation and usually ended up with a bit of spillage—sometimes a lot of spillage, depending on how much whisky had been consumed by the man on the handle, because it was all manual. But they didn't care, they used to pack the cart as full as possible. Dad would be charged for so many bushel, which is how all that sort of stuff was measured in those days, but always got a lot more.

Dad and the old Fergie

On one occasion we had set off to get our quota when it started snowing and because the whole operation took about three hours we never really noticed the weather getting worse and by the time we set off for home the wind had got up and the snow was drifting. By the time we got to the worst bit about a mile from the distillery the old Fergie was struggling. We got about halfway through the drifts and old Fergie wouldn't go any further. We were freezing and beginning to panic but Dad kept it together. Fergie was abandoned and we waded through the deep snow. I was being a bit of a wimp and crying but I don't think I have ever been so cold in my life and I was the smallest. Luckily we had progressed to long trousers by that time and after about two hours we made it home. Mum was panicking and Dad got a good bollocking for taking us with him, as if he had much option—he would have had to pull us off bodily and lock us up to stop us. But it was good to see him getting the rough edge from Mum and not us, and he was promptly sent back the next day to get old Fergie and the draff. I tell you it took a long time to thaw out and even longer before he took us for draff again.

Chapter 9

When I was seven years old we had an addition to the family. I hadn't even noticed Mum was pregnant. Why should I? I was a boy and never got told anything. Mum got up one morning with a baby and I was the first to see it although it was a bit of a mystery to me until it was explained to me that I had a baby sister. I hadn't even noticed the bulge, although I expect everybody else knew. The new baby was called Lyn, not the name I wanted. Hiawatha was what I wanted her called and why couldn't she have been a boy, anyway? Lyn was my pride and joy. I loved her to bits and still do. She didn't want my whistle, which would have been a big sacrifice as I had spent hours making it out of a piece of rowan branch.

By the time she went to school all our cast of clothes were thrown out. I don't suppose she would have looked very smart in knee length shorts, braces, a jerkin and soleless shoes, but things had changed a bit. Lyn had a better choice of what to wear and so did we all as time passed. She had a love for horses, but Dad wouldn't hear of having a horse 'It's just another mouth to feed,' he would say, so Lyn never got her horse. Obviously Dad and Mum were getting slightly better off, but she was always the baby. I looked after

shy Lyn

her and made sure she came to no harm at school, although I was only at school with her for a few years.

Lyn, like Sis and myself, didn't just get it right first time round when it came to marriage. She left school and went to work at a farm in Rothes where they did pony trekking, so she was in her glory, but it didn't pay very well and she didn't get much pony work apart for shovelling shit. Slave labour comes to mind again. She gave that up and went to work at a pet shop in Elgin and eventually married the boss's son Fergie, who, by the way, we all thought was a bit above himself. But Lyn was happy and that was all we cared about. That is except Dad, who thought he was the bee's knees, probably because they had money. But Lyn had a good house and good horses as she had always wanted and I was pleased for her. She probably had plenty money, had a son and went to the shows with the horses whenever she wanted and seemed to have everything (but then you never know what goes on indoors.) Then she met another horsey person, who she left her supposed good life to go and live with. Dad of course couldn't see past Fergie and banned Lyn from her home and continued to visit Fergie who of course was playing Dad for a fool, going for the sympathy vote, which he got.

I'm afraid Fergie's antics annoyed us for many years as Lyn's name wasn't allowed to be mentioned in the house and Dad never talked about her. This didn't just last a week or two—it went on for over ten years. But we were a bit past paying any attention to his stupid carry on and went to visit Lyn and her new man on a regular basis because Mum wanted to know how she was getting on and didn't share the old man's views. But he wouldn't talk about it, so she had to suffer, although she did manage an odd sneaky visit now and again which he never knew about. Lyn, in the meantime, had had another son who Mum didn't see until he was about seven years old. Eventually, for whatever reason, the relationship, if that is what you would call it, between Dad and Fergie broke up. It took a few more years for him to welcome Lyn back but he did and Mum was so pleased and things got back to normal, well for a while anyway.

We kind of liked her new man and they moved to a management job on a farm close to Mum and Dad, so Mum saw a lot more of her and her grandson. But her new man couldn't keep his hands in his pockets and he strayed and eventually left Lyn for some hussy or another. Lyn was gutted but Dad stood by her this time and she got through it and married an Englishman. What more can I say? He's okay and we like him and Lyn seems happy so that's good enough for me. Dad signed the croft over to her and she has some ponies and that's that.

Chapter 10

Dad and Uncle Allie went away to Glasgow one time to the car market to get a decent car. They were gone a few days. I suspect Dad went to the Barrows market in Glasgow looking for bargains through the day and to the car market at night. Anyway the upshot was they bought a vehicle each but before they were allowed to take it out they had to prove they had insurance. That was going to take too long so they slipped out at night when nobody was looking and headed for home in the dark and made it without any bother, Dad the very proud owner of a Bedford dormobile, a twelve seated mini bus kind of thing, and Allie a good cheap saloon at half the price he would have paid locally.

me with the dormobile

The Bedford was Dad's pride and joy and we even got a trip to Edinburgh Zoo which was a very special treat. It was a long day as in those days it took about six hours to go to Edinburgh, but it was worth it and the Bedford was a bit more comfortable than the shooting brake to sleep in—there were no hens involved. They wouldn't have been allowed anyway as it was washed and polished till it shone, on a regular basis. It became very useful for going to dances. Bob was allowed to drive it, nobody else, just Bob. Even Bob didn't understand his logic there, but he didn't argue and we never had to pay for petrol ever, which was out of character. If only he knew, later!

Chapter 11

In the summer it was fishing and shooting and in the winter when there was snow we sledged every night in the dark. It was a long walk to the best sledge run—about three miles. This didn't bother us except for the quarry in the woods which was a bit dark and scary. It was okay when there was the three of us but on my own it was a quick walk, or run.

Our sledges were a bit odd but very effective. One was the car boot of an old vanguard car whose shape meant it could go in any direction. The other was an old galvanized steel bath which was very light and which could hold four people and went like a rocket. The road, when opened by the snow plough, had banks of snow five or six feet deep so you couldn't get off or run off and the run was about three quarters of a mile long coming to an end at the distillery where the road was bare with the heat and the treatment from the distillery works, so you couldn't over run. It was a long haul back up every time but worth it for the buzz coming down again at high speed. We held competitions to see whose team would go the furthest. Many a night of fun was spent sledging. We would go home soaked and cold but it didn't bother us, and of course we always managed a fag. When there was no snow we went to the malting barns where we would play for hours. This was where the barley was soaked until the small white shoots began to grow. They are the important bits that make the whisky. It was then spread on the wooden floors where it was continually turned until it was dry enough to mill. There were only two workers who did the night shift—Ackie and Tommy. They just kept turning the barley over a couple of times a night while it dried, then the day shift would take over. It was then milled and transferred to the mash tun which was a big circular tank and then hot water was added and it was mixed up by a paddle which went round the inside of the tank. After the required time the water (called worts) was drained off, and the remaining solids were the draff, which was sold to farmers in the area to feed livestock. The worts was then pumped into large wooden vats called wash backs where yeast was added and the liquid was left to ferment. It was a favourite tipple with the night shift when there was no whisky or bullins available but they spent a lot of time in the loo with very little time to get there. It was then pumped into the wash stills, which were large copper vessels heated by either coal or steam. In the sixties it was all coal. The steam from these vessels was then cooled outside in cooling tanks, which had coils of four or six inch copper pipes in them, called worms. The liquid, called feints, was then stored in a steel vat, and was boiled again in a much smaller copper vessel called a still and the liquid from that was the whisky which started to come through a spout in a locked container made of brass, called a safe and securely locked by the customs and excise, at a strength of about one hundred and twenty per cent proof. The boiling continued till the strength dropped to the appropriate strength and the rest was returned to the feint tank to be boiled again with the next batch. At that time the distillery made their own malt and there was a full team of men turning the barley in the malt barns and very often they got bother with their backs, medically known as 'mat monkey' and some had permanent stoops.

We were allowed to do what we liked and the old guys obviously liked the company but we didn't touch the wash as our Uncle Eddy had warned us of the consequences. I wonder how he knew?

When we weren't in the barns we would raid the big house gardens. The green houses were full of all sorts and the walled garden with fruit.

We were never caught but one night we heard what we thought was somebody rustling in the bushes so we made our getaway over the wall at the back and straight into a ploughed field. If you have ever tried to run across ploughing in the dark in a panic you'll know how difficult it was. We were covered in earth with falling over, so that was the end of the garden raids for that year.

Another ploy was at Halloween, we would all dress up in old clothes and a face mask and a lantern made out of the biggest neep we could find. We cut the top of and hollowed out the inside with a spoon, which was not an easy task and many of Mum's spoons were bent in the process. We ate some and put the rest in the cows' sculls. When you could see through the walls, eyes and mouth were made and holes to attach a piece of baler string to carry it. Half a candle was sunk into the bottom and lit and off you set to get as many apples and nuts as you could. Usually the candle blew out with the wind and the other drawback was we had to sing or recite poetry before we would get anything. My poem was always 'To a Moose' (mouse) or at least the first two verses. It's still all I know of Robbie Burns. I got away with it because I was so wee and cute. Then the householders had to guess who you were before you got the spoils. The bothy was always the best because they got you to duck for apples and they always had some coins on the table to share out. It was also traditional after you had been to all the houses to steal garden gates and hide them. It became a bit of a joke after a few years and as you left some of the houses their final words were 'Don't put our gate too far away now!' which spoiled the fun a bit so we started mixing them up and that caused some confusion in the morning. Our wee gang never really did anything nasty or bad it was all a bit of fun and the victims would just say

'Well, boys will be boys,' as it was all boys. No girls allowed.

When we wanted to go and play or whatever at the weekends after we had done all our chores we would ask Mum first who every time would say

'Ask your dad.' So we then had to pluck up the courage to ask Dad, who would either say

'No' which we didn't question or he would say,

'Please yourself' which we soon realised meant yes. He had funny ways of communicating.

At birthday time he never ever said,

'Happy birthday.' We would get our birthday present from Mum and head off for school and at night we had to go to Dad and say

'It's my birthday today, Dad.' And he would give us any change he had in his pocket but even then I don't ever remember him saying,

'Happy birthday.' Weird, or what?

Christmas was a bit the same. We always got our stocking filled, and a main present. One year, because we wanted a real leather football, we had to share it but that was okay because we all wanted it and Santa probably had to dig deep into his pocket to buy it. Christmas dinner was also a bit weird, we would have chicken, seldom turkey, and all the trimmings and Dad would have a steak pie. He never ate any kind of bird ever—it was to do with getting their Christmas dinner on the troop ships and the turkeys not being cleaned or cooked properly. They were never told till after they had eaten it. So Christmases were never very exciting, but we thought it was okay and I'm sure it was better than some—we didn't know any different.

So having been given the 'please yourself' I would troupe off too, usually to the Thomsons' who had a fairly large farm compared to our wee croft. It was about 3 miles away across country and we would spend hours out shooting mainly rabbits or an odd pheasant. Although we were only in our early teens we were trusted with the guns, one a .22 rifle and a four ten and a 12 bore shotgun. James, the oldest, always had the rifle if the three of us went out. If there were only two of us the four ten was left at home and Norman, his younger brother, would have the rifle. James and his brother also had to work as their dad was a big, fat, lazy git and used the belt on the boys if they stepped out of line. They used to show off the weals left on their backs by the belt at school with some pride. At least we didn't get belted, just the odd skelp round the ear. The boys had two aunties who lived away out on the hill about two miles apart and they apparently didn't speak to one another. Their names were Mary and Flora, neither had inside toilets or running water or electricity, but they always had lots to eat—home baking and carnation milk. They were nice old ladies and were very good to the boys and me. When we went shooting we always made a point of visiting one or both of the aunties, who were pleased to see somebody and spoiled us with food and carnation milk which I didn't like but it seemed to taste okay when I got it from them. I think they were two very rich old aunties and old Thomson was very good to them for obvious reasons.

In the winter there were always hundreds of white hares on the hills so the shooting got exiting until you had to carry the bloody things home—they were big and heavy. So after the first time with all the excitement and shooting too many we limited it to two or three each as old Thomson didn't allow you to leave anything behind. They ate all that was shot. I don't know how he would ever have found out but the boys were adamant, maybe it was the thought of the belt if they were found out. The ultimate disaster was when we lost the bolt out of the rifle. We had a rough idea where it might have been but we couldn't find it so we had to go home with our tails between our legs. The old man was furious and we were banished from the guns. At school on the Monday the boys were proudly showing off the weals on their backs, the punishment for the loss of the bolt, but after all was forgiven we were back shooting again and old Thomson was welcoming us with a smile and lunch and mysteriously the rifle had got it's bolt back. I never asked, and was never told, how it mysteriously reappeared.

After James left school and started working full time at home he got a bit rebellious, smoked a lot and always had a half bottle. Quite a few times Mum used to take him in to sober him up with some coffee before he set off for home on the three mile trek which involved crossing a swinging bridge and up a steep embankment. It was a few years after that that he left home to work elsewhere and I hardly ever saw him again.

Chapter 12

The other farm I used to go to was where the Forbes boys lived. It was about three and a half miles away across the swing bridge again and turn left instead of right, which was the way to the Thomsons'. They were different. Their dad and mum were really nice and used to feed me till I could hardly walk. Maybe I looked a bit scrawny! Well I was, compared to their two boys who were big and strong. These were working trips—no shooting. Willie had an ex army double barrelled 303 rifle which they used for poaching the odd bit of venison and he gave me a shot at a target. One shot was enough. It had a terrific kick and my shoulder was black and blue for ages, far worse than a 12 bore shotgun. They had an old Fordson Major tractor which needed to be hand-started with a handle and I just found it fun to watch the boys cranking the handle to start it because it sometimes kicked back which was followed by a lot of cursing from them. Their dad never swore, funny I never ever heard my dad swear either, maybe they tried to set an example? If they did it didn't work.

I could sit all day on the wing of that old tractor ploughing, harrowing sowing or whatever they were doing that day. I think my highlight was when we took old Harry Lime, a crofter who lived about five miles away, in a house only accessible by a ford over the river or over a track, through the hills on Clydesdale horseback, which they had borrowed for some reason or another. Sitting on that horse's back made me feel good and pleased with myself, a bit of a sore arse afterwards and of course we had to walk the five miles back. Billy of course had already walked the five miles there as well, but that's life. He was a bit of a home bird but was good company, as was his younger brother Gordon who used to walk the three and a half miles to our house on a Tuesday night. Then Gordon and I walked another mile and a half to the public hall to the rifle club where we would meet other rifle enthusiasts and have some practise, and in my case tuition, before shooting our league cards. Gordon was a first class shot and well up the league, whereas I was mediocre. Then of course he had to walk all the way back, normally stopping to have a cup of tea and a chat at our house, and then the treacherous walk in the dark. He never had a torch going back across the swinging bridge and along a narrow path by the riverside—too scary for me.

    I also played badminton in the hall on a Thursday night, which I really enjoyed. I was in the local team and went to other clubs for matches. I was better at that than the rifle range. It was more fun. The rifle club was very serious and virtually no laughs at all. I suppose it was a bit more dangerous and a hit from a bullet might be a bit more lethal than a hit from a shuttlecock. Our tutor at badminton was Donnie MacBain, a gamekeeper from Ballindalloch. He was very enthusiastic and a very good player but he was quite often pissed which sometimes made the evening even more fun, especially when we were playing away from home. He was a very bad loser and always looked for something or someone to blame when he lost a match. It was either his racket or his partner, never himself. I actually got so good I was invited to play in a county competition in Dufftown, which I was well chuffed about and started with great enthusiasm but got severely hammered by some cocky little shit from Buckie. So my badminton career on the circuit came to an abrupt end and I never tried again. My only excuse is that the hall was enormous and I felt intimidated by the sheer scale of the whole competition. Our hall was small and low and to get a high shot you had to aim it through the rafters. At Dufftown you could hit as hard as you liked and still not reach the roof, so that was that.

We also had a football team which I played in at a very young age, probably because nobody else would play for the Glenlivet team which usually held up every other team up in the Strathspey and Badenoch league. Playing Rothes was always a bit like the badminton in the Dufftown hall. They had a full sized pitch and a team in the Highland League so they just took the piss all night and sometimes got to double figures at our expense, securing our permanent position at the bottom of the league. We didn't have a sponsor in those days. Well, who was going to sponsor us anyway? So we didn't have proper strips to wear and I didn't have football boots. I just wore my heavy boots I wore at school, which were very effective in a tackle and quite often the opposition would shy away from me when I went trundling in with both feet.

Jim Newlands always comes to mind—he was well over six feet and strong and played at full back. I was always stuck up to the front to poach as much as possible and I always seemed to crack him on the shins with my heavy boots, causing him severe pain which in turn made him very angry. Unless I was quick enough to get away he would grab me and shake me like a rag doll and chuck me on the ground and threaten me with severe violence and even said he would kill me if I did it again. Usually after the match it was all good-natured but he didn't forget because when I left school I worked at the same distillery as him and when he saw me I could almost see him cringe as he said

'Not you, you little bugger.' We then became fairly good friends. We were the most consistent team in the league—bottom of the league and had no points! Our coach was Jockie Sheed who was a single guy who lived in the bothy and worked at the distillery. He was small and fat, and you wouldn't think he would be able to run but he was fast and sharp and would hold his own against the biggest of them and he could score the odd goal. He was funny to watch because of his shape and size—he sort of rolled about and sometimes he rolled about full of whisky.

Chapter 13

In the summer holidays I always tried to get work to earn a few quid and I always managed to get a few weeks' grouse beating where I got about seven and sixpence a day which was good money as far as I was concerned. My only other experience of money was when we got thrupence to spend at the grocer's van that came round three times a week—Birnie's van on a Wednesday and Friday and Johnny Ross on a Tuesday. That was when a penny sweetie was enormous and the best deal was highland cow toffee or nougat or even gobstoppers, which changed colour as you sucked them, as long as they lasted.

Another holiday ploy was to go and help 'Geordie the shepherd', as he was known to everybody, and somehow he looked like a shepherd. You know how horsy folk are inclined to look like or behave like horses and poultry folk walk like chickens? Well Geordie was tall and skinny and he looked like a broken-mouthed ewe, probably something to do with the sixty fags he smoked every day and he'd never seen a dentist in his life. But his dogs were a treat to watch. He was the shepherd at the big farm of Drumin run by Mrs Smith, who was a right old ogre. If she saw you even looking in her fields let alone pointing a gun at them she would get out of her car and give you dogs' abuse, which to us was a challenge and fun, so we spent most of our time shooting on her land. She never did catch us. Geordie used to take me with him to help shift the sheep as the farm was spread over a large area and the highlight for me was lunch times when we went for our lunch (or dinner—in those days, dinner was taken at twelve o'clock midday.) He stayed with his dad and mum in a cottage in a small hamlet called Teetabooty and had no running water or bathroom and no electricity, but Mrs Stewart was a fantastic cook and baker. You never left hungry. His dad had been a shepherd before him and Geordie had just followed in his footsteps, which was very common in those days. Geordie didn't drive so he went everywhere on his bicycle—even moved his sheep on the bike—so it was always a bit of a struggle to get going again after Mrs Stewart's dinners. His dad and mum always made me welcome, I think they just enjoyed seeing somebody different.

In the same hamlet lived an old woman called Packi Meg, or that seemed to be what people called her, probably because she was always carrying a pack on her back. She lived in half a house, the other half had fallen down and the roof was rusty old corrugated iron. She wore long, black, tattered dresses and had long, black, straggly hair. We thought she was a witch and she scared us. In the summertime she walked round the district with a pack on her back selling matches and sewing bits and pieces and took away any old rags in exchange sometimes. When she died and the old house was emptied they found thousands of pounds hidden in drawers and boxes under the bed, and yet to see her you would think she didn't have two pennies to rub together.

The Walkers' Baker driver, Jim the baker as he was known to us, got his dinner from Mum every Monday and Thursday, I think in exchange for her bread as he was always good at giving us a meringue or a fancy piece. More than the miserable bloody grocers would give you. We even had a fish van where, when it was available, Mum would buy cod roe, which must have been cheap to fit her budget. It was horrible, and we dreaded it. It was a bit like the custard and prunes—the custard was okay but the prunes on a daily basis (well, maybe a bit exaggerated) was awful and I can't face prunes now even if you wanted to pay me.

But there was always plenty of food on the table, Mum always saw to that and we always had a roast on Sundays. Meals were at twelve sharp and supper at twenty to five sharp and if you weren't there it was put in the grill which didn't do a fried egg or baked beans a lot of good and if you didn't eat your food you got it the next day for breakfast. Well that's what she always threatened, but you knew it wasn't going to happen.

On the holidays before I was old enough to go beating, Jim would take me on his afternoon rounds up through Glenlivet and the Braes of Glenlivet. It was good fun as Jim always chatted away and I would run errands for him taking in some of the older ladies' shopping—no more than a general skivvy (child labour comes to mind again) and when we got to the end of the round at the shop in the Braes I would be gifted with a supply of two pies and fancy cakes to eat while Jim did the shop delivery which seemed to always take about three quarters of an hour. I didn't care. I was happy stuffing my face. I never did twig, but later when Jim was eventually retired I found out that he got his tea in the shop and a few drams as well. He liked a dram—it went with his red nose. Walkers obviously didn't keep very good stock records, and there was no breathalysers.

We had hideouts in the wood behind the house, secret hideouts that we had dug out underneath old tree trunks and in each kept an old miner's lamp for light. We used to spend hours playing in and out of the hideouts at war games or cowboys and Indians with homemade guns and bows and arrows. It was always a good spot for a smoke. Sometimes we even smoked rushes when we couldn't get anything else.

The Highland games were another annual outing. Dufftown, Aberlour and Tomintoul games we would go to if we could. They were all much the same. Well, Dufftown and Aberlour were, Tomintoul was a bit of a washout some years, just the usual heavy events and pipe bands, never much in the way of light entertainment like shooting stalls etc.

My athletic career was a bit like my badminton—short lived. I competed in the two hundred metres at Tomintoul and came fourth and I thought I was fairly fast but apparently not and that was that.

Bernie the bolt won everything. He was going down in my estimations as a role model—you would think he would let his wee brother-in-law win one race, I would have to go out and work after all.

Dufftown and Aberlour were different—there were the full showies—boat swings, dodgems, ice cream, candy floss, kiddies roundabouts and lots of shooting stalls, dart stalls and all sorts of games and of course the pipe bands, heavy events and highland dancers and a lot of people, a real family outing which, of course, cost money. So we were given a certain amount of money and told that when that was finished that was it and that made you watch what you were doing. It was all a bit of a cheat really as the guns didn't shoot straight and the darts were different weights. That was my excuse anyway and I'm sticking to it. My aim was always to win a goldfish, which was always the first prize you were offered. Of course you had to carry it about the rest of the day but I didn't care, and then on the bus. Sometimes there wasn't very much water left in the plastic bag you got with the fish, but they usually made it. Sometimes they would live for a while but mostly they died in less than a week, or sometimes next day. We did have a proper fish bowl and food but the end result was usually the same, and I was always warned never to bring another one home, but I did.

One year we went to the Keith show in Willie Low's bus, where we commandeered the back seat so that we could smoke our Silk Cut fags in peace. It was the usual—gang Bob, Rob, Joe and myself. Rob had a can of lager, which made our day. We also went to the Grantown show, which was usually a bit of a washout and all I ever got there was another goldfish.

The money from the grouse beating got saved as I was a bit of a miser and still am yet, fifty years on. We would get picked up about seven thirty in the morning in an old army truck driven by my mate Joe's brother Frankie who was an ex army driver. He didn't hang about and there weren't many places that truck wouldn't go. We were then deposited at the bottom of a hill with a couple of dozen more beaters and a couple of gamekeepers, stretched out over the hillside in a straight line. You had to carry a white flag on a stick, which you had to supply yourself. Some even had old y-fronts stapled to a stick. I suppose as long as it was white or whitish it would do. You also had your piece bag with a flask of tea and a sandwich for lunch-time, when you just sat down when you were told. The gamekeeper would then blow his whistle and off we would set across the hill maintaining the straight line. If you got out of line you got shouted at so you soon learned to keep up.

After what seemed like hours the shooting would start and as you approached the butts where the shooters were waiting you had to keep your head down to avoid getting shot. It was a good, fun time as the crack was always good at lunch time, although you only got half an hour before you had to move on to the next beat. Of course the shooters had their lunch in a lodge or tent with all the trimmings and champagne, which made them even more dangerous in the afternoon. Some of those old toffs could hardly walk let alone see what they were shooting at and the beaters were just fair game and there were a view incidents over the years. Nobody died so nobody said anything.

Chapter 14

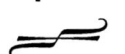

Another year I got a job lasting the whole summer holidays in the mink farm. It was a pretty smelly job and the mink were vicious little sods and you didn't need to put your fingers too close or they would have you. The food came in big frozen blocks. When a block was defrosted it got put through a big mincer, where meal was added to make a kind of mash before it was fed to the mink. You just went round with a bucket and slopped a handful onto the top of the cage and they pulled it through the mesh.

The boss was a girl called Delia. She was a big girl and I don't mean fat big, she just had big assets. She was rough, but she knew her mink and ran a very good farm. She was also scary and she had some temper—even the mink disappeared into their cages when she shouted. But she was always very good to me, work-wise I mean.

Getting nearer to leaving school I managed to convince Mum that I needed a more up to date haircut. Up till then I had to put up with a bowl placed on my head and Dad would take the hand clippers and cut up to the bowl. Sure enough it was even all the way round, but my brothers had left home and escaped the haircuts and it was only me left. Dad wasn't allowed to touch Lyn's hair. Mum took me to Dufftown to the barber's and I got a square back and sides—all the fashion then. But when we came home the old man went bonkers, shouting at me and Mum and complaining about the waste of money when he could have done the job just as well—I don't think! He went in the huff for days—you would think we had committed a crime. But it must have done some good and made him think, because he knew I was going to an interview at the college in a few weeks' time. I didn't have anything good to wear, just school clothes, so out of the blue he declared we were going to Aberdeen to get me a suit. Not just me but all three of us, the brothers that is. Great excitement! Shopping was a new experience for us, or me anyway, and we were trailed through Aberdeen

shopping with Mum, Bob must have been in Canada

where he seemed to know all the back streets. However we got our suits. The brothers got normal dark suits which he approved of, but I wanted a green checked suit with drainpipe trousers and slick jacket. It was too tight he said, but it was what I wanted, so after much arguing I got my suit and I was proud of it and Mum liked it. In fact I think she found the whole thing a bit amusing—the fact that I had got one over on the old man—first the haircut and then the suit. And guess what came next?—the winkle-picker shoes! That was the icing on the cake for me, although not for Dad. Things were looking up or he was going soft. He did grumble a lot for a while after that every time I dressed up in my new rig-out, but I didn't care. I was proud of it and wore it till they didn't fit any more. The rig-out didn't really pull the birds anyway!

He did sometimes surprise us with flashes of generosity. Like the time we were taken to Lossiemouth air display where they were taking up people in a twin winged aeroplane which I really fancied but the answer was no, as we knew it would be, because it was ten bob a time and that was a lot of money. But I kept on at him all afternoon knowing we were safe in the crowds from the usual methods of shutting us up. My confidence must have been growing having won the clothes and haircut debates (as we will call them) until he finally gave in and Ian and I were taken up in the bi-plane. It was really exciting and we thoroughly enjoyed it. I think he quite fancied it himself because he insisted he had to come and keep an eye on us. I'll never forget the views from the plane, even if it was only ten minutes round the Moray Firth and back. Just the whole landscape from the air and the colours were imprinted in my thick skull forever and it was very much appreciated.

On Saturday nights we had a disco at Tormore distillery hall. A mini bus collected us and took us home. It was all good fun. In the mini bus it was a case of who got to sit beside the girls, especially when the new doctor arrived in the glen with two gorgeous daughters who started to go to the disco in the bus. Not that they were interested in us peasants—not even me in my green suit and winkle-pickers—so it was really all in our minds.

At the disco we didn't really dance we just ran about like idiots kicking a ball about or playing table tennis, eating crisps and drinking coke while all the girls danced with each other. Rob Hendry was always playing kick about till he slipped and fell right onto my heel and broke his two front teeth. They bled a lot and I felt really guilty about it, but it was his own fault and he didn't even try to blame me. He never ever got them fixed and lived with the gap for the rest of his life. The other fashion of the day was a black polo neck under a white shirt and of course the tight trousers. We also wore a lot of brylcream to keep our hair in place.

The only girl that showed me any interest was a girl called Val who followed me about a bit but anytime I spoke to her she just giggled so that went nowhere. Then there were the MacDonald twins who spoke to me, which was encouraging since there weren't many girls spoke to us scruffy peasants, especially me in my green checked suit. Unfortunately a few years later I married one of them but that's another story.

Chapter 15

And so I left school with no qualifications, no social skills and no experience of girls. What a boring life so far. I worked my first summer back with Delia and the mink while I looked for a job. Besides, she was nicer and better company than a grumpy old gamekeeper, who's main goal in life apart from chasing grouse seemed to be chasing young girl students around the hill like a rutting stag. Worse than the Lady Chatterley's book which I believe involved gamekeepers?

Eventually I got an interview for a job as a message boy at a garage in Elgin, where brother Bob was an apprentice mechanic, and got the job. You obviously didn't need any qualifications to ride a bike. The head store man seemed to take a liking to me and took me all round the streets showing me where I was likely to be going. To me Elgin was a big city, having only ever been there an odd time. The main place seemed to be the bus station. So I had to leave Delia behind and start my career, on a bike. My wage was two pounds twelve shillings and sixpence (two pounds sixty five pence now.) You would be lucky to get a cake of highland cow toffee for that now. My digs were two pounds a week so I was left with twelve and six to do me the whole week. Mum gave me ten bob every Sunday to help me out, if I had known then that she probably had to do without I wouldn't have taken it, but that was my Mum and I was sworn not to tell Dad or he would have gone bonkers and probably cut her housekeeping money which she told us in later years was ten pounds a week. That was for feeding and clothing the whole family and feeding his large family if they came visiting, she got no extras.

I had to deliver parcels on my bike, which had a huge basket on the front and was not very well balanced when full. There were the usual capers that went on when a boy started work, like getting sent to another garage or store for a sky hook, or for elbow grease and the worst—getting covered in underseal which was like black bitumen. But there was no point fighting it because after the introduction was over nobody bothered you again and you became one of the boys. I soon got to know Elgin like the back of my hand and enjoyed my job which was mainly taking parcels to the bus station to go to other Ford garages, no brains needed.

I stayed in the same digs as Bob and they were rough to say the least. Bill was a taxi driver and drank and gambled and Elaine drank a lot as well. They had three girls, too, younger than us who we (or should I say Bob?) used to baby-sit for quite a lot while they went out or she went out while Bill was working. There was always food on the table, so they were good digs. But what did I know? I was only fifteen and had no idea about real life.

Dad never sat me down and told me about the birds and the bees. I had to find out for myself. Sometimes I wish I hadn't.

Chapter 16

My career as a message boy only lasted twelve weeks. I had seen an advert in the paper for an apprentice coppersmith. I had learned to read by that time by the way. Although I didn't have a clue what a coppersmith was I applied anyway. I was invited to an interview and to meet Willie MacLauchlan the head coppersmith. We hit it off straight away and I got the job. The wages were five pounds ten shillings. I was rich, or so I thought! Better still Mum got me digs at my great Auntie Jean's for thirty bob (shillings) a week. I now had four pounds a week for myself. Mum didn't need to give me a handout every week and although I tried to pay her back the money she lent me, she wouldn't take it. But that was my Mum—always giving and never taking. As long as we were okay she was happy. Even Dad was pleased for me as in those days an apprenticeship was what was expected of most sons unless they were bright enough to go to university, which really wasn't an option for me.

The Glenfiddich and Balvenie distilleries were run as one, both owned in those days by Wm Grant and Sons, no relation unfortunately. They had all their own tradesmen; two engineers and an apprentice, a plumber who was my uncle Stanley, a brickie who was a small fat Irish guy and possibly the laziest man I ever met in my life but a good laugh and just lived for his drams, and a labourer Dougie who was just as lazy but dour as they come, a really strange combination except when it came to drink. Our workshop was an old shed and we only did maintenance work when I started.

All pipework in a distillery is copper, it's to do with the flavour and contamination, hence all domestic water pipes were copper before plastic came along. A lot of work was done on a forge where the copper was heated till it was red hot and then worked on metal dies, or if you were doing pipe work the flanges that joined the pipes together were heated on the forge and then braised when everything was red hot. The workshop was fairly basic with only a stand drill and forge, cooling tank for tempering metal and cooling the copper, electric saw which was essential when doing pipework and pipe bender. The stills for making the whisky were getting old and worn and a lot of time was spent patching holes on the sides. Because of the demand for whisky the bosses would only close down the still for as short a time as possible, so the still would be emptied and hosed down to cool it, then you had to strip to the waist and enter the still to work. But you could only stay in a few minutes before you had to get out again, avoiding touching the sides as they were extremely hot. A still-man was always posted at the hatch with a water hose just in case.

Eventually the powers-that-be decided to replace the old stills but instead of buying new ones they decided that they would build us a new workshop and we would make them because the Glenfiddich stills had to be a special shape and size as they were only eleven hundred gallons, whereas other distillery's stills were two and a half thousand gallons or more. It had to do with the taste and quality. In fact they started heating them with steam instead of coal at one time because it was more efficient, but it changed the taste so they went back to coal.

There were three of us in the workshop. Willie was the boss. Dennis was a labourer at the beginning and was later given a class B qualification in coppersmithing because he hadn't served his time but was a very good and skilled worker although for some reason he disliked me and would cause trouble for me any chance he got. He always wanted to be the centre of attention, a show off I would call him. You would think I didn't like him, but he was okay sometimes. It was usually as the day went on and as the drink took affect that he would get stroppy. It was a bit of a shame really. It kind of spoiled my apprenticeship time as we were at one another's throats on a daily basis much to the boss's disgust. Of course as I got older I began to retaliate and eventually left before I floored the git, which came close a few times, but not before I became a fully qualified coppersmith having served my five years apprenticeship plus a one year probation to go on a full wage—twenty two pounds ten shillings a week. Coppersmiths were one of the highest paid tradesmen at the time. Maybe that was what annoyed him, the fact that I was going to be a fully qualified coppersmith earning more than him and always would.

The new workshop was quite a luxury. Not so much the equipment as it was all second hand, but it worked. The sheets of copper came flat and cut to size and we then had to get them red hot on the forge, carry and place them on a metal die, clamp them to the die and then beat them into shape with big homemade wooden mallets. Everything was done manually. The copper fumes and dust were everywhere because every time you heated the sheet another scale of copper would peel off when you started beating it. It probably took a day to every sheet, so it was hard work and hot work. No face-masks or goggles in those days. Once the sheet was in shape it was washed with Vitriol acid, which came in big round glass bottles. Again, no protection except for rubber gloves. And to complete the process the sheet had to be plannished (hardened) which was done by feeding the sheet over an electric hammer. It took three people to hold it and the pattern had to be right. The sheet weighed about one hundred and fifty kilos so it was hard work as it wasn't for ten minutes, it was a whole day or more per sheet. Welding the sheets together was done by oxygen and acetylene gas. One person would weld on the outside with a big torch applying the welding rod and the other would be inside with a smaller torch pulling the weld through, ensuring the weld was the same thickness as the sheet. It was then plannished to harden the weld. Again the apprentice (normally me) was put inside the still to hold a one hundred kilo steel weight against the weld while the other two, one with a flat hard steel tool held against the weld and the other with a twelve pound fore hammer, hitting it as hard as they could. This sent shock waves through your body as you bounced about inside the still holding on for grim life as you had to have it back on the spot before the next contact. Not a word was spoken throughout this process as sheer concentration was required, except if you weren't on the right spot and the dull thud triggered some abuse aimed at you because when that happened the hammer swinger would lose his momentum and miss the tool and bash the soft copper. When that happened there was normally a stop called for everybody to cool down and the two outside would swap over, but nobody ever swapped with yours truly on the receiving end inside. When I had finished my time I was given an apprentice, Michael, who was a bright sixteen year old and quite normal by day and picked things up very quickly and although I don't know what ever happened to him after I left, I'm sure he was going places. Outside of work Michael was into flower power, which was all the rage in the late sixties and early seventies and he could be seen wandering the streets in his flowery robe. He took a lot of stick at work, but he didn't care, as he was then the new boy on the inside and I was let loose on the outside welding and using the hammer or the plannishing tool. That was progress but it wasn't as easy as it looked. Your timing had to be perfect, but then when you got on the hammer it was never your fault if you missed, it felt good.

Most of the other parts were made in sections and shaped by hand by heating and then working the copper with special hammers to stretch the sheet to the shape required. It was a very satisfying job as you could always admire your workmanship every time you went to work, and the faults of course, but only you knew where they were. Every now and again I would get a cash bonus when Willie would just hand me thirty to forty quid and just say put it in your pocket and say nothing. It took me a couple of years, because I was a bit thick, to realise where the money came from. Willie would load up all the scrap copper in his wee

A40 van and meet with a scrappy somewhere out the road and that was where the bonus came from. Copper had a high scrap value in those days.

At that time distillery workers were entitled four drams a day—one at eight o'clock, one at twelve when you went to lunch, one when you got back at one o'clock and one at five o'clock when you finished. This was dished out by the brewer and if you had a leaking still or some horrible job you got another to revive you. Mostly it finished you for the day. It was clear whisky about one hundred and ten per cent proof, half a tumbler full which turned blue when you added water to it as I did but some of the older guys drank it straight. You could feel it going straight into the bloodstream. I think we must have gone home pished most nights but nobody noticed as they were all pished as well.

We had a few ploys for getting whisky. One of the ways was from the pipe coming out of the worm tank, which carried the newly condensed whisky. The pipes were joined with flanges, which were bolted together using five-eighths steel bolts on which the nuts had to be welded for the customs and excise to stop theft, or so they thought. We would cut the bolts short just allowing enough to attach a nut to tighten the flange and then weld a piece of bolt into the other end of the nut to make it look as though it was welded. So when we wanted whisky we just slackened the nuts and filled a bucket and hid it under the saw bench where it was never found and the customs never ever discovered the scam.

Another ploy was when we weren't very busy we would get sent into the warehouses to tap the barrels of whisky. This was the method for checking the contents by tapping the side of the barrels with a small wooden hammer and you could tell how much the barrels had lost by the change in the tone from hard to a hollow sound. Of course you soon found out where the best barrels were. They were normally the casks that had been full of sherry before and they were usually the ones that were a bit empty. The method of stealing from the warehouse was by hanging a dog (a piece of inch and a quarter copper pipe about nine inches long and an old penny which fitted exactly into the pipe and was soldered in place, the other end was shaped to take a cork bung and two lugs braised on it to tie on a piece of string) which was then hung down the trouser leg to carry it into the warehouse, dropped onto the best sherry casks to fill. Then you put the bung back in and carried it out the same way. The reward for being the manufacturers of these items was to get the first fill of the dog. On the odd occasion when somebody was caught with a dog the manager would always come to us as his first port of call, but we had no idea what it was and had never seen one and we certainly didn't make them. Being caught meant immediate dismissal.

The manager at that time was a man called Duncan who had worked his way up the ranks. Nobody knew why he became a manager but he was a right little fat Hitler. Of course he knew what a dog was, he had had one made when he worked in the warehouse, but he could never catch us making them.

In the sixties Freemasons, or the Goaties as we used to call them because they seemed to worship a goat, were a very close-knit society and had many members in the local community. In fact I think that's how Duncan got up the ladder so quickly, he was devoted to the Mason Lodge. There was certainly evidence that if you wanted to get on in your career it was a lot easier if you were a Mason, especially in the distilleries and also in the police apparently.

Dennis, my tormentor, was a Mason, although it probably didn't expand his career because he was such an obnoxious little shit and posing as a goat would have been appropriate for him. Half way through my time the management harassed me to join, it would help me in my future I was told, and I was eventually persuaded to attend a meeting. All that day Dennis was supposedly priming me how to behave and the rules of the lodge, but in the end I didn't go, it just wasn't me, posing around dressed as a goat and taking all the secret vows and learning the golden handshake, which I never ever could understand. And anyway I was never any good at keeping secrets and there was no way I was going to worship a bloody goat. I wasn't asked again and I felt a bit left out for a while as most of my mates were in them. So their secret was safe. It's a lot of rubbish anyway and a good excuse for a booze-up and it was men only, which was a bit scary.

Chapter 17

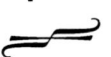

My time as a coppersmith wasn't a very healthy time. Working on a forge all day meant every time you heated the copper another scale would come off and when you were beating the sheets you were breathing the dust, so I ended up with big boils on my back and neck and millions of blackheads and was often ill with a flu type illness caused by the copper content in my blood, the doctor said.

My digs at Auntie Jean and Donald's were cheap and okay and I just lived as one of the family. Gordon Villa, as the house was called, had been bought when they retired from a farm they had on the outskirts of Dufftown. It had three stories and I was up at the top, which was fine as you then couldn't hear the rows as poor old Donald got told off once again.

There was one other lodger, Geordie MacPherson, whose family belonged to the third and last house in Teetabooty. Geordie was quiet, went out only a couple of times a week. If he did drink too much you could always tell because his face was always bright red and had a permanent grin, unlike his brother Jockie who lived in the family home at Teetabooty. He was a pain in the neck and the only time he came to see his brother was to borrow money. Geordie never went home–who would blame him? Jockie was always drunk when he came and Jean hated him. She didn't stand fools easily. She would give him dogs' abuse and wouldn't even give him a cup of tea. A couple of times I witnessed

Jockie being removed from the premises by the scruff of the neck and told never to come back. But it was like water off a duck's back and whether Jockie didn't or couldn't remember he always came back for more.

His son Lennie also stayed at home. Lennie was a big lad and liked his drink and food. It was amusing to see Lenny eating—especially soup. The only reference I can make is to a JCB, the spoon never stopped till the plate was emptied. Maybe it was Jean's soup? It was always potato soup which was okay, but she always put what I think must have been gravy salt in it to thicken it. That made it a disgusting brown colour, and I have to admit I struggled to eat it sometimes. But to leave it would have been criminal, and I can assure you the plates weren't small.

She always gave me a couple of rolls with cheese on them every day for my piece. The rolls weren't bad, a bit hard some days, but edible. The cheddar was green and not edible and I had to throw it out and just eat the rolls. Apart from that the digs were fine and I really enjoyed staying there. Well it was cheap and the price never went above thirty bob.

Donald had had an operation on his mouth. It was a cancer of some kind caused by pipe smoking, but he was still smoking and had acquired a habit of spitting. I don't think he could help it, to be fair. He had a spittoon to spit into which sat on the tiles but he seldom hit it. He spat in the fire against the fire-place and even the dog wasn't safe if it sat in front of the fire. Old Jean used to shout at him to watch what he was doing but Donald didn't care where the next one went splat against. Donald was also the message boy. He got sent out for the daily shopping but sometimes he would get blethering to somebody and not come back as soon as instructed and another row would develop. I even witnessed him getting the frying pan over the head when she'd had enough, although it was usually a newspaper. She was a big woman and Donald was a small skinny man who walked with a stick. He wasn't scared of her and the language was unrepeatable. He wore rimmed glasses with thick glass—they were like looking through a magnifying glass.

When their daughter Gertie came to visit she was big but very jovial and always laughing and she mollycoddled me like my mother did. She took over the cooking while she was there—that was a treat. She continually baked and I got fresh bread and ham in my piece box. I wouldn't have trusted Jean to put ham on my piece, not that it was ever to happen.

I had a lot of bother with my teeth in my youth and had to attend the dentist for fillings and extractions. Eventually when I was sixteen, Dr Rae decided they would all have to come out to try and get rid of the abscesses, and it definitely wasn't with eating sweets. Dr Rae was well over six feet tall with a mouthful of silver fillings that looked rotten and he looked like he needed a good dentist himself. Struggling wasn't an option—you were pinned to the chair by a supposed nurse who was built like a tank and there you stayed. I can still hear and feel that bloody drill as he drilled big holes in my mouth trying to get at the abscesses. It was almost a relief when he declared defeat and I was booked into the hospital.

On the declared day I strode into the Dufftown Hospital expecting to get an injection in the arm and I wouldn't know a thing about it. But no, I got gas to send me to sleep, if that was what it was supposed to be. A mask was placed over my face and I was pinned to the table breathing in this horrible stuff, head spinning and drifting in and out of consciousness. I felt every tooth coming out and every time I moved they just pumped more gas into me. I eventually woke up in a room on my own with not a clue where I was and a very sore mouth. Eventually a nurse came, helped me up, led me to the door and wished me farewell. My head was spinning as I wandered up the street and I'm sure people I met would have thought I was under the influence. Well I was, but not with what they thought. I was never so glad to see Gordon Villa in my life. Jean gave me a drink of water and sent me off to bed where I stayed, I think, for three or four days, only waking for a drink and a plate of saps (bread and milk mixed) now and again.

It took about three weeks before I could go back to work. I was continually sick and the taste of gas wouldn't leave me. Even yet, forty seven years later, I still cringe and can taste the gas when I think about it. You didn't get your new teeth for about six weeks by the time they took impressions and made new ones, so I didn't venture out much in that time. I wasn't a pretty sight. A lot of teasing went on at work and I definitely didn't attract any girls. I can still picture Dr Rae the big git and he has joined my list of life hates, after Dennis. I don't think it will be a very big list but we will wait and see. But I had the best smile in the end.

•

Chapter 18

Dufftown was a bit boring for me as I didn't know very many folk apart from relations and I didn't really want to see them so I decided to get mobilised and bought a scooter—a Vespa scooter in fact—costing all of ten pounds. But it was quite old and had a few problems, like the brakes didn't really work and the front wheel wobbled. But its main problem was it would only go about three or four miles and then stop. The needle in the carburettor kept sticking, cutting the flow of petrol, but you got used to it and sometimes a thump on the side of the bowl worked or you just screwed the bowl off and on again and it was good for another four miles. It was handy in town to go and come from work and for going home to Mum's marvellous home cooking for the weekend. But I soon traded it for a Lambretti scooter, which was much smarter and I knew I would get to my destination without getting covered in petrol. I paid twenty quid for it and got five pounds trade in for the old one, so I was quite happy.

I passed my motor-bike driving test when I was sixteen, which meant I could have bikes over one hundred and fifty cc although I never did. By this time Bob had got a Morris series E car and we had started going to dances, mostly in Edinvillie and Aberlour. They had Saturday night dances week about and we could get ten people in it.

Bob's next car was a big black Ford Consul. It was a real beauty and held even more folk. Being a mechanic Bob was always under the bonnet doing whatever mechanics do. He even took the engine out one time and rebuilt it, fitted a new clutch and put it all back together again, all in one weekend. And it worked. Of course in those day you could work at cars, not like now when you nearly have to have a degree to lift the bonnet.

Mum, Ian and Lyn

teenagers and cheeky Lyn

Bob, favourite cousin Tish, me, Lyn and the rat catcher, and Bob's pride and joy, his Ford Consul

me and Mitch and that dog again

Ian had started coming home on leave and always brought a bottle of dark rum. We used to get a bottle of coke, pour half of it into an empty coke bottle, top them up with rum and nobody was any the wiser. We weren't drinkers so it was a new experience for us, or me anyway, and I didn't take that much. But we all smoked, in fact it seemed everybody smoked except Dad in those days. I think it was the second time Ian came home with his rum that I overindulged and in the middle of the night I felt very ill and the world was spinning. I had to make a mad rush for the bedroom window to be sick. Unfortunately we slept upstairs and I didn't think of taking out my teeth so they shot out the window with the sick. Suddenly realising what had happened I shot downstairs and scraped about in the dark in the sick for my teeth, much to the hilarity of Bob and Ian watching from the window. A quick swill under the tap and back to bed thinking nobody would notice. But old hawk-eyes Mother was shouting up the stairs in the morning demanding to know who had been sick. She couldn't miss it, having slipped on it in the dark on her way to milk the cow. It was well spread out as it's a long way down from an upstairs window on a windy night. Nobody ever owned up, no grasses in our team. I have never touched a drop of dark rum since that day—even the smell makes me feel sick like the gas did.

After a few outings to dances I eventually asked one of the twins to dance. It had to be a slow dance as I was never a bobber. I could do the twist but never really felt comfortable doing it and felt a bit stupid having watched other boys trying their best and looking daft, and them knowing that we were all watching and taking the piss. It really put you off. We were worse than girls for taking the mick out of each other. The girls at least danced with each other and there was no way the boys were going to dance with each other, well not then anyway.

Chapter 19

So being mobilised on my old scooter and with my old, thick, kaki army coat on I used to go round to the twins' house nearly every night, anything to get away from the spittoon and the risk of getting spat on. Esther was the lucky one who fancied me and I have to admit the feeling was mutual. Her mum and dad didn't seem to mind. Her dad owned and ran the local coal merchant's, Big Hugh as he was known. Hugh was big and again I mean well over six feet and strong as an ox. He had an old Thames Trader lorry to deliver the coal but all the rest of the work was done by hand and his shovel was enormous. It took something like about four shovelfuls to fill a one hundredweight bag. He had a weighing machine but seldom used it, just now and again to check. It was always near enough. Then the bags were loaded manually onto the back of the lorry. I, on occasion, got roped into the filling of the bags which he seemed to do more at night when I was around. It wasn't exactly what I wanted to do when I went courting but I didn't argue. I think he maybe took advantage of the situation because I wouldn't have liked to be on the wrong side of him. He was a good crack anyway, and I quite enjoyed working with him. It also helped build up my puny muscles. Sometimes I would go out on the deliveries with him, especially to the braes of Glenlivet, which could take a whole Saturday.

Norman of Achavaich farm always springs to mind. I never knew what his last name was—he was always known as Norman of Achavaich. He was like a gentle giant, wouldn't say boo to a mouse, which is just as well when you saw him move sacks of coal. He could do a lot of damage if he had a temper. He lived with his mother at the very top end of the Glen. There was no road for the last four miles, just a track across a ford (river crossing) and up through fields and bogs not fit for a lorry, so Norman would meet us at the ford and the coal bags were transferred to a trailer towed behind an ancient Fordson Major tractor which had seen better days. This was no effort to me as I couldn't match or keep up transferring the bags so I was a spectator. We then had to go on the trailer to the farm so that old misery Hugh could get his bags back, or that was his excuse. Hugh liked a dram and there was always plenty at Achavaich. Norman's mother, old Meg, was a nice old lady and could keep Norman in line, and there were always plenty of scones and cakes to go with the tea. To my surprise and Hugh's amusement she opened a drawer of the sideboard and offered me a slice of porridge. It was something I had heard about but never seen. It was more common in bothies where the single farm workers stayed. The farmer's wife or the servants would make a big pot of porridge on a Sunday and pour it into a drawer and the workers would just cut a slice for breakfast or even a snack. Needless to say I refused, scones would do me fine, as soon as she cleared the hens off the table and the cats off the chairs to get a seat. They possibly didn't get many visitors away out there, so anybody who did visit got the full works and you didn't leave hungry, or sober in Hugh's case. So Hugh was in good form when he left and the lorry always seemed to know the way home. Unlike some folk, Hugh got cheerier with whisky and never shut up, and we were to enjoy a lot of pints together in years to come. He never did let me drive his lorry—I think maybe because it was new and it was his pride and joy. I would have been the same. It was a pity because when they introduced HGV licences there was a concession that if you had been driving a lorry for over six months you didn't have to sit a test, and you automatically got your HGV driving licence. Norman on the other hand became like a friend and if you met him in the local pub, The Pole Inn, he would buy you drink whether you wanted it or not. He was a bit like a minder. If you met him at a dance he would watch out for you and nobody argued with him, as gentle as he was.

The Pole Inn was run by Jack and Madge and many a good night was spent in the small bar. Jack was very often merry but I never saw Madge the worse for wear. You had to play darts through the crowds as the bar was only about three yards wide and about six yards long and always busy. Nobody left sober and a lot of the farmers (as the Pole was the only bolt hole for many miles) quite often got run home by Madge. There was never any doubt about closing time. Madge would appear with the three foot sweeping brush and start at one end and by the time she got to the other you were out the door, finished or not. There was no give or special cases—you had been given the ten minute warning to drink up and that was that. Even poor Jack got abuse if he argued, which he seldom did.

There was a character called Beets (Boots) I think so named because he wore heavy tacked boots with no socks and he was always covered in oil as well as his clothes. He looked like he hadn't had a bath for a long time and he used to go to the Pole. He lived in a caravan and drove heavy machinery in the forestry somewhere and earned his beer money by drinking old engine oil for a bet. If he was really hard up he would swallow a mouse or two, washed down with some old engine oil, and of course there was always somebody willing to take his bets, especially tourists who had never seen the likes before and probably never would again. It wasn't long before Madge had him banned and Beets was never seen again. His engine probably seized with lack of oil.

Anyway, Esther was the only girlfriend I ever had and after a couple of years brother Bob started going out with her sister and eventually we all got married on the same day when I was only the ripe old age of twenty. Bob was in the RAF so he didn't need to worry about a house and Esther and I were given the use of Hugh's father's house at Drumnagrain. His father had been a blacksmith and when he died Hugh had kept the smithy and the house. It needed a lot of work to make it habitable, especially due to the lack of a toilet and bath. I had seen septic tanks before so I had a rough idea how it all worked. So I dug a hole about four feet square and built it up with blocks and put a separation wall in it. Although it was all a bit slap dash it worked well enough for us. Having worked with copper it was easy enough to plumb it all in and we were soon up and running. It was somewhere to live even although the toilet was in the wooden porch with no insulation.

Chapter 20

As soon as I was seventeen I started driving lessons and went every Sunday afternoon for a lesson in Grantown-on-Spey with Mr Duncan from Aberlour. He would pick me up and I would drive to town and go around the streets for a bit before he dropped me back. Grantown wasn't a very big town, maybe half a dozen streets, but they did driving tests there and he had a new Volkswagon beetle car, which was more suitable than my old Morris Minor. I was proud to be a car owner and would, even now, have a good old Morris Miner, but they were never really met with any enthusiasm by any of the wives or bide-ins I had over the years. Well not yet, still time . . . .

We seemed to buy all our cars from a garage in Dallas, a small town about twenty miles from home. Sandy Thomson owned the garage and he was an old crook but we kept going back thinking we were getting a good deal and he always made you feel like you were. Dad knew him well, but the Morris was fifty quid, which I didn't have, so after a lot of moaning the old man gave in and loaned me the fifty quid which he made me pay back over the next ten weeks. Surprisingly he didn't charge interest.

I was proud of my old 1954 Morris Minor and couldn't wait to pass my test so that I could discard my old army coat which wasn't really a bird puller. But disaster! I failed the first time, concentrating so hard that I didn't notice the fading white line at a 'give way' sign and drove straight through. I nearly died when I realised what I had done and said to the examiner,

'That's that then; is it?' But the frosty faced bugger just said,

'Carry on, Mr Grant,' and he made me complete the test. Then I was handed the piece of paper with the fault marked on it and

'I'm sorry Mr Grant you have failed.' And he got out and disappeared. Mr Duncan wasn't too chuffed with me either and in those days these folk didn't mince their words, so I booked a new test, which I got in about three weeks and I sailed it. It was a different examiner who actually chatted and smiled so I felt a bit more relaxed.

That was me, on four wheels! I gave up my digs at Donald and Jean's and I think they were genuinely sorry to see me go. I moved back home much to Mum's delight, not sure about Dad. But I did do my bit about the croft which was better than sitting watching telly waiting to see where Donald's next spit was going to land. I drove to work every day and had my lunch in the Glen café which was run by two Robertson sisters whose father had the farm of Rennettan up the Glen.

Kate was the older and always made you welcome and there was always a laugh. She wasn't pretty, but nice, and at that time in her early twenties. Her sister was a bit younger, very pretty face but a bit plump. The food was good. I reckon her mum taught her as it was all farmhouse food, fresh and tasty. Kate made the best soup around and the café was always packed at lunch times. She also had some nice young waitresses, especially Jill, who did a bit of flirting. But ach, she was too giggly and I was too shy, so that went nowhere and my Morris didn't do anything for her anyway. Esther liked my Morris. It was more pleasant going round to her place at night and sitting in a car rather than standing about in the cold with the scooter. After the old green Morris Miner came the blue Morris 1000 followed by a Mini. The Mini was the aim because it was cool to have a Mini. I had traded the Morris Minor for the Morris 1000 and then that for the Mini with the old shark Thomson. The Mini was a bit of a heap and didn't get much encouragement. At home there were some comments about me being done, as in ripped off, but I had a Mini and I was proud of it until the sub frame broke in two. It was a common complaint in the earlier Minis but I was determined and found a second hand sub-frame and with a little help, or maybe a lot of help from Bob, we soon had it back on the road. I decided it needed a paint as it was a very dull white, so I bought some blue paint and a paint brush and painted it, much to the amusement of all other family members. They thought I was bonkers. But it looked good, well at least when it was moving, and a bit streaky when stopped. And of course, when I went back to Thomson's to look for another he gave me next to nothing for it because it was hand painted.

My cars were getting better all the time. I bought a Ford Popular, which I had always fancied but I didn't like it much. It only had three forward gears and I found that it was very high geared and you had to be at a certain speed to get to second gear and the same again to third. You really struggled on a steep hill if you lost the momentum.

So, back to old Thomson. We were really getting to know each other by now and I'm sure he rubbed his hands together with glee every time he saw me coming. I bought another Mini a bit newer this time, a red one—it was smart and boy could it go. It knocked ten minutes off my time going to work every morning and certainly raised my street cred. It was a good buy for a change and didn't give me much bother. Minis were great winter cars, they could plough through snow—drifts, which I had to do a lot in the winter as the glen between our house and work was always filling up with snow. I think these were some of the first front wheel cars and it seemed to give more traction although not on ice—they were useless and I had many a hairy moment spinning round with no control, waiting to see where I stopped. The other advantage of the mini is you could lift it out of a ditch if that is where you stopped.

Chapter 21

Now that I was earning a reasonable wage I could buy my own clothes. My dress sense was improving—well I thought so anyway. Having grown out of my green suit I had moved on to denim jeans and I bought myself a new jacket, a Jacob's jacket as everybody called it as they took the mick because it looked like the coat of many colours Jacob wore, as in the bible, and I can assure you it had nothing to do with my religious beliefs. But I loved that jacket and wore it with pride. Mum didn't like it and when I did get another jacket it was leather, well imitation leather, and my super jacket of many colours mysteriously disappeared. It had gone well with my black polo neck and white shirt. Come to think about it I don't think there is even a photo of me wearing that jacket. After I passed my test I was suddenly in demand for lifts to dances and I used to go and pick up our pals. Rob Hendry was working on a farm away in the hills in Morinsh and it was a bit rough. They didn't treat him very well. He slept in the loft and had a couple of heavy coats on top of his bed to keep warm at night and he wasn't very well paid. Rob had to walk three miles to meet up with us to get a lift and he always arrived with one of the big army coats which was packed into the boot for going home again. He used to claim that it was the only time in the week that he was warm—when he got into the car. Needless to say he didn't stay there very long. The other mate we used to pick up was my school pal Hamish. He was a year younger than me.

He had started taking epileptic fits and his mum would only let him go with us because when he sometimes took a fit on the dance floor, although it all looked a bit alarming to other people, we knew what to do and it was a case of, 'Oh no, here we go again.' His sister always came as well so she normally dealt with him. By the way, she was one of these snobby clever clogs that snubbed us at school—changed days now that she needed a lift. One of the other ones was even worse and very clever and left school with every qualification she could get and then fell foul of the sixties social activities. The third one did do alright and went on to be a highly qualified teacher of some sort but was still a snob, and still is.

There were so many of us going to dances that Dad would lend Bob the Dormobile. You can only get so many folk in a car, so the Dormobile was more suitable. Dances at that time always finished by twelve o'clock (no dancing on the Sabbath) but you never got home that early by the time you had finished your carry out as there was no point in taking it home as Mother thought we were all good little boys and Dad would have gone bonkers if he thought his blue eyed Bob had been drinking and smoking while driving his beloved Dormobile. The bobby (policeman) didn't seem to bother either if he saw you all piling into the Dormobile. He would just wish you a safe journey home and tell you to drive carefully. Well we did sort of know him a bit.

But I needed a bigger car, so the Mini was traded in, to guess who, Thomson of Dallas, for a bright red Austin A40 with a black roof. It was a beauty and I was well proud of it. I even managed to drive all the way to Greenock with Esther for a holiday with her Granny Rose who was a nice old soul. This was before we were married, but all very proper, no hanky-panky and separate bedrooms. Granny Rose made sure of that, but it was good fun and we even managed to get on a ferry and spend a day in Rothesay and enjoyed the beach at Largs. Granny Rose was good company. Esther's Uncle Davy was a bit weird though. He was always sneaking about and interfering in everybody else's business and talked a load of rubbish, a bit of a know all who knew very little. I didn't like him much. Maybe he could join the hate list.

Typical of my luck, two weeks before we got married we were going to the sales room in Elgin to buy furniture and it had been snowing and the roads were icy. Going through Aberlour I skidded and pranged my bonny car into a tree and bashed the wing in. Although we managed to knock it out it was never the same again and I traded it for a green A40 with a black roof at, where else, Thomson's. It was a good wee car, not quite as flashy as the red one but getting married meant the car wasn't quite so important as I had pulled the bird.

Chapter 22

So Bob and I got married to the twins. I have to be honest and admit I can't really remember much about that day, nothing to do with drink or anything, but I'm sure all the uncles and aunties had a good time especially Auntie Adie. All I remember is that Mr Malcolm the minister who was partly blind performed the service and the reception was in the Aberlour hotel and it didn't cost me anything, which was important. Brother Ian could have been my best man. Bob's mate from the RAF was his best man. Elsie's friend Linda was her bridesmaid, but I can't remember who was Esther's bridesmaid. Maybe it was my sister Lyn, and maybe brother Ian was my best man. I'm sure if they ever read this I will be corrected, as will my family enlighten me on any other mistakes when, or if, they read this. I had promised to join the church as part of the deal, and I can't even remember if I did that or not, but the outcome was that I was married, and I was quite happy about it, and things were picking up. I'm sure everybody enjoyed themselves. I'm afraid that's all I can tell you about that, I wonder if Bob can remember?

With hindsight we were far too young and life wasn't easy for the first few years. We didn't have much and a Sunday roast was a lump of stew roasted. A common meal was curried eggs as we got them for nothing from the in-laws. I'm afraid the curried eggs go on the hate list—they were disgusting.

At the distillery when you were eighteen you were allowed to get your daily allowance of whisky, which in my case, never really having had much experience of alcohol, was a bit of a novelty. Between that and getting topped up with our pilfered pure alcohol from under the saw bench meant driving the fifteen miles home at night was sometimes a bit of a struggle and sometimes a blank. So a few months after we were married and I had completed my years required probation and received my certificate I decided it was time to change my career.

I think my decision was helped along by the near destruction of poor old A40 one morning on my way to work. On a very winding part of the road just before Aberlour I met two Russels of Bathgate artic lorries who would have been on their way to a distillery with malt grain from the plant in Dufftown and they were trying to pass one another on a corner. I didn't have a chance. It was pitch black and pouring rain and all I could see was four headlight spread across the road. The outcome was inevitable—I hit the lorry on my side of the road and caved in the wing. I was a trembling wreck and couldn't move for a few minutes until I realised what had just happened. The two lorry drivers were quick to see if they had killed me or not and accepted full responsibility and, I liked this bit, pleaded not to involve the cops as they would probably lose their jobs and maybe their licences. So details were exchanged and I was told to report to the depot on my way past into work.

But that wasn't the end of my morning nightmare. Down to one headlight I proceeded towards Aberlour and met a convoy of army armoured cars. And I mean met them, head-on, because of their limited vision they thought that because I had only one headlamp I was a motor bike. The collision took my whole wing out and bent the track rods. I think the driver got as big a fright as I did. After much deliberation I decided it wasn't worth chasing the army as it sounded too complicated and to just blame it all on the lorries, which I did and the company didn't argue and I got my good old A40 back looking as good as new, well to me anyway. What a morning!

That certainly helped me to think of a change in direction. I was becoming aware of my alcohol intake and probably so was the wife although she never ever said anything. Seeing the state of the people around me, some relying on it and getting the shakes if they couldn't get it, scraping about at night in the dark emptying the dregs out of supposed empty barrels (and some of that stuff was poison I can assure you.) Then there were those who didn't drink at all and enjoyed a full social and married life. I knew some families where the wife would be waiting in the pub on a Friday night for the husbands to come with the wages and most of it would be spent by eleven o'clock on drink and one arm bandits, and some wives whose men went straight to the pub and spent the wages before they went home on a Friday night to abuse their families. These wives usually had another source of income to pay for food and clothing for the family.

The Duncan brothers always come to mind. They didn't drink. They were both stillmen (the men who operate the copper pots that make the whisky) one at Glenfiddich and the other at Balvenie. They were real family boys, very sporty and they took it very seriously. There was great rivalry between them, both played football, golf and badminton. Losing wasn't an option—what a contrast between them and the ones that lived for their drink. I couldn't believe how far Willie could drive a golf ball. It was a serious problem in the distillery world all over and I didn't want to get into the rut and sink with the rest.

Chapter 23

Suddenly our life changed dramatically when our first-born arrived. Graham weighed in at nine pounds ten ounces. Esther had to go all the way to Aberdeen to have him and it took her twelve hours. Luckily I wasn't there, wives were just left to get on with it in those days. So now we really needed a decent house. I decided to try my hand at farm work and applied for a cattleman's job at Deskie with Mr Gill and got it. Everybody thought I was mad. My wage was five pounds a week less than I got at the distillery, but I got a free house, a ton of coal per year, half a ton of potatoes and milk, so in my book I was better off especially with the house—a cottage with a proper bathroom. There was no damp to be seen anywhere.

The hours were long and I don't think I had a weekend off in all the time I was there. This meant overtime, which would have been fine if Graham hadn't kept us awake all night. We even had to resort to taking him out in the car for a run till he fell asleep and then gently carry him to his cot. He was a right pain in the arse. He wouldn't keep his food down but the doctor said he would be keeping enough to keep him going and eventually he settled and never looked back. Esther's sister had a baby about a month before, being identical twins they seemed to do everything together. Well nearly everything. When Bob was posted abroad Elsie spent a lot of time staying with us, which was okay as it kept Esther happy and took the pressure off me. There's nothing worse than a bored woman. So I was better off and just ten minutes from home and, although it was hard work, it was healthy.

Mr Gill and I hit it off straight away. There was no Dennis to irritate me on a daily basis. There was a grieve (foreman) employed as well and he did most of the tractor work and had little to do with me, luckily, as he was a lazy git and was inclined to shy away from anything that involved hard work. Gill was very pernickety and everything had to be done his way. Fair enough, but it was always the hardest way. There was a big wooden cubicle shed that held fifty cows, it was called a mootel, cattle courts to hold another seventy, a small court for younger stock and a byre that had twenty five cows tied in it. That was the first job every morning and last thing at night, and I can tell you twenty five cows can produce a lot of shit in a day. I thought the four cows at home were bad but this was something else, although good for building the puny muscles. All the silage had to be loaded by hand although there was an electric cutter for cutting the silage in the pit. Large four wheeled barrows were then used to transport it to the cow feeders. It took all morning to feed all the cows and load up the troughs for the afternoon.

I still played a bit of football and badminton and could get a game of darts when Bob came home on leave and we went for a pint. Mr Gill taught me a lot about cow management over the next two years and my confidence grew. In the meantime Bob was posted to Kinloss, about thirty miles away, and when Elsie stayed with us I used to go and fetch Bob and take him up to our house for the weekend and run him back on a Sunday night. Bob didn't have a car at that time because he was being moved about by the RAF.

In the meantime I had again visited Mr Thomson whose three sons were beginning to learn the car trade, or how to con people out of their hard earned money. I bought a Ford Cortina, another improvement with lots of room in it. I really wanted to get a Ford Capri but could never stretch to that, and never did. A few weeks after getting this super car I had to run Bob back to Kinloss on a Sunday night, taking the two boys of about two years old with me for a run. On the way back just after I had passed Mum's house and about a mile and a half from home I fell asleep and rolled the car, and ended up upside down over a dyke. Luckily the boys were tied in and they didn't even cry. They just sat there upside down wondering what was happening. Well I knew what had happened and I got a terrific fright, dragged the boys out and walked the couple of hundred yards back to Mum's. Dad had heard the crash and was on his way to see what had happened, not realising it was us. After settling the kids with Mum we got old Fergie out and rolled the car back onto her wheels, towed her back to the croft and stuck it out of sight. Dad ran me and the boys, who didn't seem bothered by the whole crisis, home, where I was not a popular boy. That was the end of the good old Cortina and me out of pocket as all I could afford in insurance was third party.

It was back to the Thomson's, again. They must have made a bloody fortune out of me over the years. The only cheap thing they could offer was a Zephyr four. Petrol was getting dearer and so these bigger cars were hard to sell. I was a bit desperate and we didn't really do that many miles, especially since Graham started sleeping normally. I was banned from taking the boys on my own and no more runs to Kinloss. Well it suited me. The Zephyr was a luxury to sit in and drive, very big with a long nose. I soon got used to it and loved the sheer size. It made me feel good.

After about a year and a half I felt it was time to try and move on and get a bit more responsibility so I applied for a head stockman's job at Scottish Malt Distillers farms at Birnie beside Elgin. I didn't know at the time but they had several farms spread from Elgin to Keith and up country to Knockando. All the farms were attached to distilleries owned by SMD. The farm manager invited me to an interview and he was nothing like Mr Gill who, especially when at the market selling cattle, wore his oldest, torn and dirtiest clothes he could find so that the buyers thought he was a hard up poor farmer and would pay a wee bit more to help him along. He never smiled even when he was getting a good price. I have to admit I adopted the same method in later years when I was selling and it does work. But not Mr Mair. He was a collar and tie man and never got his hands dirty and the interview was very official. But he was okay and knew what he was talking about and asked all the technical questions to which I didn't really know the answers as Mr Gill didn't really go in for the technical stuff. But I bluffed as much as I could, as I did on nearly every job I applied for, and then he passed me on to the farm grieve, Bill Petrie, to show me around. I was to be responsible for the suckler herd amounting to about one hundred and twenty cows and the fattening cattle in the cattle courts. It seemed straight forward and a different system from Mr Gill's. The wages were good and I was to be in charge of the stock. So interview over I was told they would be in touch, as they do, and I thought that was that. I returned to my silage barrows.

About a fortnight later I got a letter from Mr Mair offering me the position as head stockman at the home farm and we moved two weeks later. Mr Gill was not amused and tried to get me to change my mind even as we were loading up the cattle float with our furniture. But I had set my mind on the move upwards.

Chapter 24

It was a completely different set up. There was Bill the grieve, Geordie Thomson (no relation to the car sharks) the tractor man, and his mate Tosh a qualified mechanic who drove the other tractor and old Davy Sutherland who was somebody who did whatever needed doing and just seemed to be passing time to retirement. He was a quiet man but had an endless knowledge of stock and helped me a lot. I liked him a lot. He never said a bad word about anybody. Bill was new like me and had a bit of a hard time when he started because Geordie's father had been the grieve before him and Geordie expected to step into his shoes but was bypassed in preference for some new blood. There was a fair bit of back stabbing in the early days as Bill made a lot of changes that Geordie didn't like and there was a lot of friction and criticism, but Bill rode the storm and eventually they all got on.

Geordie and Tosh's tractors were always in perfect condition. They spent every spare minute adding more lights or washing and polishing them, I hadn't seen anything like it, and when it came to ploughing time it would take them anything up to two days making sure the plough was straight and leaving even furs before they would start. Me, I just used to stick the plough on the tractor and go for it and the ground got black just the same. I was never allowed to plough in the same field as them.

We had a good semi-detached house and our neighbours were Geordie and his wife Carol. They had two boys and also two lodgers, his mate Tosh and another young guy called Gerry who was a bit of a loose cannon. He worked in Elgin somewhere and quite often came home drunk, not that he bothered us but you could hear the heated discussions through the walls as the kitchens were back to back. The result of the activities that went on next door was that their kids swore a lot and the only time I ever had to reprimand Graham was when he started copying the other boys. Every second word began with 'f' or 'c', but not being used to severe rows he stopped and I didn't hear him swear very much after that. We weren't really a swearing family, well not at that time anyway, and I had given up the drink.

I enjoyed my work and there was very little hard labour. If a tractor could be used to make life easier, then it was. The herd of cows were good. Mr Mair bought good quality stock and at calving time I would keep a round the clock watch even going out at midnight for a look. There was a Mini pick-up, which I was allowed to use to career around the calving field. It was also very good for catching sick calves, when Geordie or Tosh would drive and I would dive on top of the calves on the run. The boys thought I was mad but it was fun and effective. It wouldn't have been approved of by Mr Gill. He would have been tut tutting.

Fiona was born while we were at Birnie, without any bother, and in fact she never was any bother, not like Graham. She slept all night and we sometimes thought there was something wrong, it was bliss. After I had been there about a year I was going to work one morning and my face felt a bit funny but I didn't bother much until Geordie saw me and after a good laugh said he thought I should go home and call the doctor. By this time my face was getting a bit sore. When I went home and looked in the mirror I could see where the amusement was coming from. My face was huge and Esther got the doctor who confirmed I had mumps and to expect the next couple of weeks to be a pretty painful experience and he wasn't kidding. It was the most pain I had ever felt.

I couldn't get away from it and it didn't only affect my head, which was even worse. I was pretty sick for the next three weeks and we didn't want any more kids anyway.

In the summer I got promoted to other duties on the farm and at harvest I got introduced to an old New Holland combine and sent to cut barley. Basic instructions were given and off I went. I got to like the combine once I finally conquered it and ironed out the teething problems—not the combines, mine. First time I emptied the grain into the trailer I forgot to retract the spout and because it was beside a wood I caught the spout on a tree and broke it off. Well I thought that was it, my combining career over before it had really started, but Bill just said 'Don't worry these things happen.' So the spout was repaired without any fuss. Mind you there was a lot of hilarity and leg pulling for a few days by the two worthies Geordie and Tosh.

It only took another two days before my next disaster when I was changing gear, which was always a problem because it was stiff. The gear stick broke off and I was left holding it like a right idiot. Again it wasn't a big problem and Tosh soon fixed me up and off I went. Of course by this time I was the butt of all the jokes at work and at home, but I didn't care, I was enjoying my new experience. I managed the rest of the season without any more major disasters apart from nose diving the cutting table on the front of the combine into the ground on a hill in the dark. The lighting on my old combine wasn't that good. I wasn't allowed to stop at night as long as the crop was dry enough. I had to just keep going, as cold as it was, because there was no cab on my machine, until Bill came and stopped me. Geordie was nice and snug in his modern cab.

I must have been doing okay because I got sent on the main road without an escort (nobody seemed to bother at that time) to a place called Tarrycroys. It was about twenty five miles away. The header of the combine didn't come off so it was twelve feet wide and on the main Elgin to Aberdeen road. I was told to keep pulling off the road to let traffic past but I soon got fed up with that, otherwise it was going to take all day to get there. The forward speed was not very fast as it was, so progress was slow, and got even slower when the police pulled me over and ticked me off for not stopping enough to let the traffic past. When I eventually got there, I could see why Geordie didn't want to go there. It was only fields of barley and some cattle, who were grazed there in the summer. Trailers had been left in the fields, which somebody emptied at night, so I never saw a soul all day. Boring or what! The novelty of being a combine driver was fast diminishing.

I was also the fertiliser spreader, which I at first thought was a great honour until I saw the pile of fertiliser. A stack of two hundred tons in one hundred weight bags was a bit of a thought but the spreader took a ton and a half and had a self-loading device so it wasn't so bad but again there was a lot of travelling to farms out and about.

They grew a lot of potatoes and that was old Davy's domain. He planted all the potatoes with an old two-row planter. It took him weeks to get through them. When it came to lifting I was promoted to the digger and two busloads of women lifters from Dufftown were brought in. They were a tough lot. I soon worked out why I got the digger job. Every time you went up the drill you got dogs' abuse, you were either going too fast or not fast enough or 'We're struggling, give us a hand!' Or it was just plain rude remarks that didn't do your ego any good. It was a nightmare and then to top it all off they went on strike at lunchtime demanding another fifty pence an hour. So Mair, who was obviously hiding somewhere out of trouble, was summoned to sort them out which made him very nervous. It was okay bossing us around but when it came to sixty odd unhappy women he just melted like butter in their hands and they got their fifty pence an hour and he got a lot of abuse and called things I'm sure he had never heard before. But they did come back the second day and finished the job, which was his biggest fear. It certainly had an effect on him because the next year the automatic potato lifter appeared, which didn't argue back.

Chapter 25

There was a new distillery built at Tomnavoulin in Glenlivet and they were looking for shift workers so in a moment of madness I applied. At that time we weren't getting on that well with our neighbours, they seemed to have taken a dislike to Esther for some reason or another, probably because she didn't join in on the booze sessions. We got a new council house in Tomintoul which had been allocated to the distillery for workers. It was just a few doors away from Auntie Ellie and Uncle Dougie so I was able to see Dougie a lot more which I think he enjoyed as by that time he couldn't talk but managed to communicate in other ways and could hear perfectly well.

The distillery work was different and easier. It was eight hour shifts which changed every week. My job was in the dried grains department which involved filling about seven or eight bags every hour. On the night shift it got very boring as there were only another two men working, a stillman and a mashman. On my shift there was a loud mouthed English guy who knew it all and was always half way up the manager's arse looking for promotion, but it didn't get him anywhere and he was still in the same job long after I left.

Being a new distillery it was nearly all automated so not a lot to do. A mini bus took you to your work so you didn't even need to drive. In the summer the distillery closed down for about four or five weeks to do annual maintenance so you were on day shift cutting grass, painting and tapping barrels in the warehouse. It didn't take long to find the best barrels, but the method was slightly different this time. Instead of a dog in your trouser leg it was an empty half bottle on a string down each leg. They had to have cork tops to allow for a bit of expansion. It was a bit cheeky but nobody seemed to care. On one occasion, while standing talking to the manager outside the warehouse, I could feel the whisky running down my leg and could see a puddle forming around my feet and old Fraser just laughed and said,

'Better go and sort yourself out before you pee yourself any more,' and little did he know I nearly was peeing myself with panic. That was it, I never did it again and he never ever mentioned the incident. He didn't have to. He could obviously see the shear panic in my face. Anyway I had about twelve bottles in my cupboard at home and I didn't even drink it.

I had plenty of spare time being on shift work so I used to go fencing with the local fencing contractor, Jock Farquharson. It helped to get me out from the heat and dust I had to endure at the still. Bob used to come too when he had time off. Jock never seemed to be short of work and employed all sorts of worthies and paid in cash. Bob and I could fence a bit anyway as we had helped Dad on the croft. Jock would mark out a fence and give me and Bob a spade and a punch and leave us there all day, sometimes digging strainer holes while he would supposedly go to price another job. He would appear back about four o'clock, plastered, and probably never got past the first pub or had found a pub on his way back because he always got the work. Jock didn't need to say a word, you could tell straight away by the grin and his eyes seemed to nearly pop out of his head when he had a drink. But he was a good crack and hard worker when off the booze. We could complete three hundred metres a day and he taught us how to swing a mell (a big flat-headed hammer which could weigh eight or twelve pounds, used for driving fence posts) properly. Jock's were always twelve pounders and the art was to just keep going round in a circle using the bounce off the post to help the next swing. Not a very good description and I couldn't show you now but it was a lot easier than lifting the mell from the ground every time. We soon got the hang of it. We were sometimes left to our own devices when we would never see Jock for days, we just presumed he was at another fence, although we had our doubts. But he always arrived to measure the finished fence and pay us.

I arrived at a fence one day and there was a new man started, Jimmy Riddich. He had met Jimmy in a pub over the Lecht at a popular watering hole of Jock's called Briggies. It was a small hotel frequently used by the hardy folk that lived in the hills of Braemar, and the odd tourist if they had the bottle to enter. After a bit of barter where Jimmy claimed he could mell posts all day, Jock had challenged him to give him a demonstration never thinking he would see him again. But drunk or not Jimmy was there ready to start on the Monday. Jock was small but strong and Jimmy was well over six feet and built like a tank. He wore heavy tackety boots, no socks, an old tattered kilt and a semit (sleeveless vest.) He had a big mop of curly ginger hair and face full of freckles—a scary piece of work to look at but had a very quiet voice. It was even more scary when he swung the mell as he was a true Scotsman. But he was true to his word—he could swing a mell. Where it was taking Bob or me five or six swings to put a post in Jimmy took three at the most. Even the cars had to stop for Jimmy when he was in full swing, if he was working on the road-side. And so Bob and I got demoted to staple duties and trying to keep ahead of Jimmy punching holes for the posts. When you got to know him he was quite a nice person and was full of stories about his encounters with drink, the police and experiences inside. I never asked questions. Any information was given voluntarily at piece times.

We became good friends over the next few months. Always on a Friday night he would disappear back to where ever he came from. Sometimes he wouldn't turn up till Tuesday and sometimes not for a week, which used to irritate Jock. But when he was there he certainly earned his keep. The last time I saw him he said

'If you ever need somebody sorted, I'm your man,' and that Friday Jimmy disappeared and I never saw him again, neither did Jock, but he was one of these people you never forget and I sometimes wonder whatever came of Jimmy.

Jock's wife Joey kept him in line, or she tried to. One time Jock was in hospital getting sorted out he asked me if I would keep things going and left me a fence to put up at Delnabo just outside the town of Tomintoul which I did and we became very good friends. After that, if Esther was at Elsie's I would get my dinner from Joey when we were finished for the day. That is up until the time Jock had gone to look at a job and came back mortal. He arrived at the house just at the same time as me and his eyes were just about to pop out of his head. When I looked at Joey her eyes were even bigger. I had heard Jock referring to Joey's headlamps but I had thought of something else, but I knew now what he was talking about. Jock was literally thrown upstairs and I was told to sit down for my tea, which I did smartly. I could hear Jock singing away upstairs while Joey threw my dinner of trout at me with never a word spoken and I quickly made myself scarce. That was scary, but next day Jock was his old self as if nothing had happened. He probably couldn't remember anyway or he was used to it. After that I politely refused any offers of kindness. I had a lot of fun with Jock and will always cherish my memories of him.

Chapter 26

I soon got fed up with the distillery and took my twelve bottles of whisky, which by the way I never told Jock about, otherwise he would have been a regular visitor till it was all gone, and headed back to Mr Gill. He was looking for a farm grieve and when I phoned him about it he didn't hesitate. I was heading back to where I had begun except to a different house. I didn't have as much cattle work to do this time but I was allocated the new Ford 7000 four wheel drive. Now that was a good tractor and I did most of the tractor work which meant getting out and about a bit more. After a bit the cattle man left and there was just Gill and me so the days were long and I was back on the silage barrows until my brother-in-law hassled me for a job because they had hit hard times and Bernie couldn't find work. So eventually I convinced Gill to give him a try. Bernie was a good worker, nothing was any bother to him and they were glad of the decent house. He had a wee bit of a problem having me as his boss and telling him what to do, but we got on okay. They stayed for about a year and then moved on to Tomintoul. He was replaced by a supposedly experienced cattleman who talked a good job but knew nothing, had a bad temper, wouldn't work overtime, and his stock care was crap. He just wanted the money. Now Gill wasn't into sacking people but after an argument on the silage pit he tried to hit Gill with a grape (fork) which wasn't very clever as I had seen Gill in action fighting with a big Limousin bull, and the bull lost. So he was thrown off the silage pit and sacked on the spot.

Mr Gill had been fighting with his landlords for many years and it was beginning to come to a head and although he was confident he would win nobody else was. He was a stubborn old bugger and wouldn't negotiate with the estate. I was beginning to feel a wee bit insecure so I thought it must be time to move on again.

Chapter 27

Dell Estate on Loch Ness was looking for a grieve so I applied for that. Charlie Smith appeared at my door one day at lunchtime, which was a bit uncomfortable as I could see Gill up in the yard and he asked me afterwards who it was and I just mumbled something about insurance. But a month later I was history. I think he was sorry to see me go because we did get on well, and it wasn't everybody who got on with Gill.

Dell Estate was different again. All the cattle were outside and I had full responsibility for the day-to-day management. Charlie had responsibility for the whole estate and trying to keep old Lord Bradford happy, which wasn't easy. He was of the old school and expected to be called 'My Lord' and all workers were expected to dock their hats when they met him and address him 'My Lord.'

'No way,' I told Charlie. He wasn't my lord. I wouldn't and I never did, not that I saw the snob that much anyway. He didn't communicate with us mere peasants, and if I did meet up with him I just didn't address him in any way and he didn't complain. If Charlie was around you could see him cringing. He probably had a snigger afterwards at my contempt, or poor old Charlie got it in the ear. Part of my duties was to milk two cows, which was a real pain in the arse. The farm was expected to supply milk for the big house and all estate workers. They all had their own metal buckets, which Charlie collected every morning and delivered, making sure his lordship had his milk for his breakfast.

Charlie was a good boss and never interfered with the day-to-day running of the farm. His wife May kept him in line. She did the paperwork and I think they actually ran the estate between them although he was the front man. May was a very cheery person until she was annoyed with somebody and I can tell you she didn't take many prisoners. We all became really good friends and anytime you went near their house you always got your cup of tea and cake. When Charlie had taken over the management of the estate he had met with a lot of local resentment as the glen had been run by the Macpherson family for many years and they had made life very difficult for a bit. Rory had been the estate manager, his wife Effe had been doing the books for the estate, his brother Ian had been the gamekeeper and another brother Wolston had been given the only farm tenancy on the estate on a lifetime tenancy agreement. The estate game income had been almost non-existent as the Macphersons had been selling for their own gain. They were the wealthiest family in the whole glen and kept the local pub in business. Rory and his wife also ran the local post office and I can't begin to imagine what went on there. Wolston was probably the worst farmer I had ever seen. He was drunk on a daily basis and if I was unlucky enough to meet him he was abusive to me and always tore strips off Charlie. It was even a thought to go into the post office because of the frosty reception, and I don't think I was in the pub more than four times in three years because nobody spoke to me.

They were obviously a wee bit put out by the new regime. Ian the gamekeeper had been sacked and a new one employed. Alistair wasn't much of an improvement as the Macphersons soon had him in their pocket. He liked 'the drink' as they say in the west and was sometimes to be found trying to hide from Charlie in the woods supposedly spying and locating the whereabouts of the deer. To be fair, when sober he was an extremely good stalker and did know where to take paying guests for the best roe deer or sika stags and an expert at snaring foxes—probably why Charlie put up with him even if he couldn't find him half the time.

The tractor man, Douglas, was a bit of a geek and was awkward from day one as he thought he should have been the new grieve and he told you so any time you had an issue to argue about. Again Douglas 'liked the drink' so that was when he usually started his moaning. His tractor skills were non-existent even although he had a new Ford tractor to perform his duties with and we soon developed an understanding that as long as he did what he was told we would get along fine. He had a wee boy also called Douglas who he used to take in his tractor, which I had to stop because his lordship had complained to Charlie, and Charlie said it was my responsibility to deal with the matter, the coward. This meant that his wife Sheila stopped talking to us as well. They left about a year later, Douglas having found a management position in Invergarry, God help them.

There were only about one hundred and fifty sheep on Dell and apart from my time helping Geordie at Drumin when I was a boy I had never touched a sheep in my life. I had lied again and bluffed my way to Dell. After I applied for the job I had read a bit about sheep so I could talk a wee bit about them and obviously Charlie was impressed or he thought I was a real idiot. It didn't take long to get the hang of it and Charlie who had a good knowledge of sheep helped me along and I even managed to shear the tups, which nearly killed me. We got a contractor to do the ewes, but being a small flock it was a bit of a dawdle. But there was something missing—a dog.

I got my first dog, Tess, who was to be my bread ticket for many years to come. Charlie had been at the mart one day and ran into somebody who was selling ready to run dogs, so he had gone home with him and bought this young dog who already had the name Tess. He called at the house that evening, which he did most evenings because we had become really good friends over the months and he had been teaching me about management and I had started record keeping. Anyway he produced this dog who had a half white face and we all fell for her. Tess became one of the family. Whatever kind of life she had before, she was now stretched out in front of the fire and soon made herself at home. She became my daily loyal companion, turning into a very good and classy sheepdog and there was a great deal of local interest in the prospects of pups from her, even the Macphersons wanted one. Everybody said a bitch always settled better after they had a litter, so Tess was introduced to a top trial dog at Tomatin and in time produced five pups. I sold four and wanted to keep the fifth as he was a big bonny dog and started running with his mother at a very young age. The manager on the neighbouring estate kept pestering me to sell the dog and so when the money got big enough I did sell and immediately regretted it.

Chapter 28

The second winter we were there we had an enormous snow-storm and it was minus twenty six degrees. Even the water coming into the house was frozen. We had to carry the bales of hay out to the cows on our backs as even the tractors couldn't move. It wasn't easy, we tried using the agro-cats but even they struggled. The sheep who were sheltering in the woods were getting frozen to the ground and big snowballs were forming around the bottom of their fleeces and they couldn't stand up, so we spent many hours and days clipping snow from the fleeces as it wasn't very difficult to catch them.

The main road was blocked from Fort Augustus so there were no food supplies and after a week a helicopter came along and dropped us a loaf of bread and half a pound of butter which was supposed to keep us going for a week. Luckily we had plenty of potatoes and we had recently killed a wedder hogg (young male sheep) between Charlie and ourselves and Alistair had given us a bit of venison. But after a couple of weeks we were getting a bit fed up of mutton and Esther was running out of different recipes. Eventually a bulldozer started clearing the twenty five miles of single track road between Fort Augustus and Inverness. When it was about five miles from our road end they realised they were going to run out of diesel and the road had filled in behind them so we got a call to see if we had any fuel left, which unfortunately we had. I made two trips carrying five gallons at a time on my back through the deep snow. It took three hours each time. I wouldn't like to try it now. But it kept him going until he reached our end of the Glen and he even cleared our drive, although only, I think, to get more fuel. Seeing the bulldozer brought me back to my childhood. All this time the Macphersons and co were watching out the pub window and nobody ever said 'thank you', except the bulldozer driver. Three weeks is a long time without fresh food, although we did have milk I suppose, but we soon got back to normal.

As well as Tess, Graham spent all of his time, when he wasn't at school, sitting in the old Zetor tractor. For some reason or another all these cheap communist tractors had a passenger seat, It didn't matter what I was doing he was there, even gathering stones when his uncle Bob was visiting. I had just ploughed a ten acre field that hadn't been ploughed for twenty years, and it was covered in stones. It took us a whole week and Bob has never forgotten the stone field, or his back didn't anyway. He was lucky he didn't work with Mr Gill—we once spent three weeks on an eight acre hill reseed gathering stones, but I think he was obsessed. It was boring, day in day out, Gill had a few odd ideas or maybe he didn't keep moving with the times. Another was cutting thistles round the edges of fields with a scythe when the job could have been done in no time with the grand new topper sitting in the yard. But he wouldn't hear of it.

Almost every Tuesday Charlie and I went to the auction mart in Inverness, sometimes I would take stock in a float behind the MF 135 it was the fastest tractor on the road, and it took about an hour to cover the twenty miles. I soon knew all the back roads into Inverness, avoiding the traffic. Charlie always bought me lunch and it was always mince and tatties with a scotch pie on top. It was delicious and sometimes if Anne's not watching I still manage to sneak a pie on my mince.

I bought my first cow in the Inverness mart. She was a big blue grey cow with twins. I had my eye on her all day and Charlie thought she would be a good cow, so when she came into the ring he prompted me to bid and she was mine for three hundred and fifty pounds. The auctioneer knew I was keen on the cow and I'm sure he knocked her down a bit quick. I was well proud of myself that night taking my own and very first cow home in the float. Esther didn't say much and wasn't very impressed, but the kids were and I would worry about paying later, as I always did. In those day the market would give you a fair bit of credit and you just paid when you sold the calf or in this case the two calves. Unfortunately the cow got an infection in one of her front foot clefts and the vet had to cut it off. I had to cowp (turn her over) her every day to change the dressing. This involved putting a rope round her neck in a half hitch then one round her chest in a half hitch and then one round just in front of her hips in another half hitch and if I stood behind and pulled the rope tight it put pressure on her heart and she would go down and I could then work at the foot with ease. It sounds a bit gruesome but it works perfectly well and is quite safe for the animal. After a couple of weeks it healed perfectly and was never any more bother and I doubled my money when I sold the calves.

George, the vet came from Inverness and became a very good friend and would come and castrate and dehorn the calves. On his second visit he asked me if I wanted a shot. I think he was joking but I said,

'Aye, why not?' So instead of getting kicked to bits in the crush I got what I had always thought was the easiest bit, but of course nothing's easy. But I mastered the job and although I couldn't do it all the time because George would probably have got into trouble, it came in handy in later years. My training as a coppersmith was beginning to come in handy as well because we didn't just weld copper, we were trained in fabrication and welding steel, oxygen and acetylene welding, braising and also on burning equipment. Dell estate had a very well equipped workshop with a pit so I got to do most of the repairs and maintenance on farm and estate machinery.

Charlie was beginning to make noises about my possible ability to manage on my own, and him having sown the seed I started looking for management positions although I was happy where I was and Charlie would be kind of sorry to see me go as I was an ally he could depend on and I had become very fond of him and May.

Also, of course, going against all the medical theories that once you had mumps you were infertile, Keith made a late appearance and was born in Inverness. So our responsibilities had increased and we had to think very carefully about our future.

The kids were also well settled in school. Ian and Dalsie MacAskil ran the school bus, or the car in their case. Ian had a small farm at the top of the glen and a small lorry with a float on the back and was often seen at some odd hours transporting livestock of some sort around the country-side. He was a short, fat man and always had a big grin, which got bigger as the day went on. He liked the drink, and sometimes you would wonder how he ever got home as the lorry looked like it belonged to the hotel. But he was nice with it and wouldn't do you a bad turn, in fact the opposite. Dalsie was a big girl and didn't take many prisoners, you always knew where you stood with her as she would call a spade a spade and no messing, but gentle with the kids and looked after them as if they were her own, and hated alcohol. She drove a Lada Riva, which was the Russian version of a four wheel drive and they were built like a tank, a bit like Dalsie herself.

I was watching the Scottish Farmer for managers' jobs every week but they weren't plentiful. There was one at Alvie Estate at Grantown-on-Spey which I applied for and didn't even get a reply, so that wasn't very encouraging. A few weeks later there was an advert for a farm manager on the Island of Colonsay which I applied for, even although I didn't have a clue where it was. I had, over the years, obtained good references so my applications looked reasonably good.

A few weeks passed and I had kind of forgotten about it when there was a knock at the door. We were all sitting having one of our chats with Charlie. I answered the door and there stood this kind of scruffy man with a fair belly on him and an old, battered, blue Volkswagen van. My first thoughts were, 'scrappy', but then he introduced himself as Paul Hobhouse and that he was here to interview me for the farm manager's position on Colonsay. I felt very uncomfortable inviting Paul in while my present boss was in the house, but what the hell, there was nothing I could do about it, so we all sat and finished our tea. Charlie and Paul conversed about farming and then Charlie made his excuses and left. He was no fool. Paul stayed for ages and we had a long discussion about stock and of course I had a wee bit more knowledge of sheep. By the end he was inviting us over to Colonsay to see what it was like and left us to think about it.

'Colonsay wasn't everybody's cup of tea,' is how he put it and he wanted somebody who would stay as he had gone through quite a lot of managers over the last few years.

Next day Charlie was in the yard early and just asked how I got on—I told you he was no fool—so I just told the truth and he wished me luck and said he thought it was time to stretch my wings and go for it and if Paul wanted to phone him he didn't have a problem with it. Not many people with that kind of attitude.

So on the fifteen of March nineteen seventy nine we went on an adventure into the unknown, got to Oban to catch a ferry, the only other ferry we had been on was to Rothesay a few years before. It was the SS Claymore and there was a gale brewing. It wasn't a pleasant trip and the two older kids were sick all over the place and Esther was very sick and wasn't going on a boat ever again. Keith and I were okay. He didn't really know what was going on since he was only six or seven months old, and it never did bother me that much anyway. We eventually arrived at Colonsay pier and were met by Paul in the old van and taken to the hotel where we were to stay for the next two days. It was freezing. The hotel owners Kevin and Christa had just taken over the hotel the previous October and were just settling in and the heating didn't work very well. Esther had already made her mind up, there was no way she was coming to stay in this dump. I kept an open mind and when Paul took us on a tour of the Island the next day I kind of fell in love with the place and she mellowed a wee bit. She was taken back to the hotel and Paul and I got down to the serious business of looking at the livestock and discussing wages and conditions and the future farming policies as it was a bit of a mess and really needed sorting out. It was not farming as I had been shown in the north and I had a lot of good ideas. He was impressed and offered me the job that day and suggested I discuss with the wife when we went home.

The next day we were shown the house on the inside, I had seen it from the outside the day before and thought it looked okay. But the wife was not impressed when she entered Kiloran—in Dell she had a nice house, comfortable and modern. Mum's housing dilemma came to mind briefly that day. But Paul made all sorts of promises to improve the house before we moved in and, well, I went away reasonable happy but I could see I had a bit of work to do on the wife before she was convinced. We left the next day on the ferry and headed home. I having made my mind up that was where I wanted to be. We talked about it long and hard and weighed up the pros and cons and eventually Esther decided to give it a go. I told Paul and we were given a start date of the fifteenth of May. Charlie was well pleased for us although he would be genuinely sorry to see us go and wished us luck in our future.

A cattle float was organised, which was the normal way to transport farm workers furniture and things, and on the fourteenth of May nineteen hundred and seventy nine we set off on a very eventful future and adventure for the next twenty seven years on the Island of Colonsay.